John Coltrane

Already published volumes in the
JAZZ MASTERS SERIES
Count Basie by Alun Morgan
John Coltrane by Brian Priestley
Duke Ellington by Peter Gammond
Gil Evans by Raymond Horricks
Dizzy Gillespie by Raymond Horricks
Coleman Hawkins by Burnett james
Woody Herman by Steve Voce
Billie Holiday by Burnett James
Gerry Mulligan by Raymond Horricks
Charlie Parker by Brian Priestley
Oscar Peterson by Richard Palmer
Lester Young by Dave Gelly

Forthcoming volumes will include:-
Ornette Coleman by Barry McRae
Miles Davies by Barry McRae
Stan Getz by Richard Palmer
Benny Goodman by Bruce Crowther
Jelly-Roll Morton by Peter Gammond

JAZZ MASTERS SERIES

John Coltrane

BRIAN PRIESTLEY

Discography by
Brian Priestley

Apollo

First published in Great Britain in 1987 by
APOLLO PRESS LIMITED
11 Baptist Gardens, London NW5 4ET

British Library Cataloguing in Publication Data
Priestley, Brian
John Coltrane.—(Jazz masters series; 9)
1. Coltrane, John 2. Jazz musicians—
United States—Biography 3. Saxophonists—
United States—Biography
I. Title II. Series
788'.66'0924 ML419.C645

ISBN 0-948820-02-0

Series editor: David Burnett James

Typesetting by Concept Communications, Crayford, Kent

Printed and Bound in Great Britain by
Anchor Brendon Limited, Tiptree, Essex

Contents

Illustrations

The publishers thank Roy Burchall and *Melody Maker* for access to their files.

Chapter One

'He was really involved in music. It looked like about eighty-five per cent of his life was music. I mean, he really never was satisfied. He was always looking and searching. He had this undying appetite for continuing to look for something different, and challenging himself all the time.' These are the words of McCoy Tyner, pianist with the John Coltrane Quartet of 1960-65, describing its leader. And the particular quality he describes is what, above all else, inspired those who were associated with him or followed in his footsteps. 'He had tremendous influence on our music, and a sort of school was developed. Even in the rock world, a lot of those musicians grew up listening to the Quartet. As a matter of fact, in Europe they had a festival of rock musicians, and they dedicated the festival to John.'

Given the enormous respect engendered by Coltrane around the world, it is perhaps not surprising that his spiritual influence on the aspirations of others has been so widespread. But what is even more remarkable is the amount of direct stylistic influence he had and continues to have. Instruments as different from the saxophone as guitar and piano reflect Coltrane's style when they are played by people like John McLaughlin or Carlos Santana, Chick Corea or Keith Jarrett; and naturally the millions who try to emulate these performers are carrying the same torch, whether they know it or not. Of course, when it comes to the tenor and soprano saxophones, Coltrane is frequently described as 'the most imitated player in the whole history of jazz.'

Thanks to the growth in the international audience of jazz, compared to the heydays of Louis Armstrong and Charlie Parker, it is hard to deny the truth of this statement. Lengthy lists can be drawn up of established saxophonists who have undergone Coltrane's influence, but the seeming unavoidability of his style—as something which anyone must absorb, before there is a chance of finding one's own way—is striking. Mike Brecker, often cited as the state-of-the-art saxist of today, said in 1973 at the start of his career, 'If I sound like Trane on a certain thing, or if I sound like Trane all night, . . . that's just what I hear. I just let it come out.' Even in 1984, on tour with Steps Ahead and on their album 'Modern Times', Brecker paid homage to Coltrane in a tune called *Oops,* the tenor solo of which is directly modelled on the classic *Giant Steps*.

To my lasting regret, I saw Coltrane perform only once, and before I was ready for it. His European tour of 1961, the only one to include dates in Britain, found me with some background knowledge of earlier styles of jazz, but little enough to hold onto under the combined onslaught of the five performers, especially Elvin Jones. I remember, though, a long and exhausting *My Favourite Things,* and I remember a very brief ballad which (because of its key and the last two notes) must have been *I'll Wait and Pray*. I recall too that, after the concert, I was strangely elated by the music despite having understood so little of it, and also that the number of fans at the stage-door was tiny. Security seems to have been non-existent, for I was able to wander right onto the actual stage and observe the equally shy Eric Dolphy at the piano, toying with a chord superimposition (D minor on top of E-flat minor). And I could glimpse Coltrane himself in his dressing-room, surrounded by about one listener and talking with intense seriousness.

There is, of course, not only personal reminiscence but an abundance of documentary evidence to show that not many people took to Coltrane's music right away. And many of those who did develop from involuntary fascination to intimate familiarity were then caught on the hop by his apparently abrupt changes of style. But the immense amount of work that lay behind these changes, especially during the years 1956 to 1966, is naturally easier to see in perspective as the period recedes into the past. Now (August 1986) we are already closer to the 20th than the 15th anniversary of Coltrane's death, and his position as a figurehead remains as strong as ever. But there is another, more general sense in which he exerted an enormous

John Coltrane Photo: Jazz Journal International

influence over his contemporaries and successors in jazz and its related fields, by emphasising an aspect of improvisation which was almost totally new.

This element might be described as the search for enlightenment. The cellist Paul Tortelier once said during a televised master-class that 'An artist mustn't search—he must find,' thereby neatly encapsulating the European ideal of the interpretative performer at the service of a god-like creator/composer. Nor, it should be noted, is there any room (or any need) for searching in traditional African music, which is part and parcel of everyday life and ritual. That was the philosophy which, when transplanted, became the source and the strength of black music in America, and it was the creative conflict between that approach and the European ideal which gave us superlative jazz improvisers such as Louis Armstrong, Coleman Hawkins, Art Tatum and Charlie Parker—artists who found their solutions every time they played. But 'practising in public', as it was termed by Coltrane's detractors, clarified the new concept of the jazzman as someone who seeks but doesn't necessarily find, a concept which is much more closely related to Oriental music—or, at least, to Oriental music as it is perceived by the Western ear.

It was perhaps first expressed in jazz by Lester Young, an early idol of John Coltrane, and especially by Trane's last guru Miles Davis. The workshops of Charles Mingus also played their part in legitimising the idea of jazz as a process rather than a result, but it was particularly Miles's stylistic changes which provided the clearest precedent for the odyssey of Coltrane. Doubtless, Coltrane's influence in this respect was greater than any of these predecessors simply because his ascendancy came at exactly the right moment when, as Marshall McLuhan put it in a non-musical context, 'the whole world was going Oriental.' But the search for truth, or for the meaning of life, is not something which ended with the 1960s. And Coltrane's search for his style—for himself perhaps—has come to be seen as an essential part of what jazz is all about.

Chapter Two

The search for the real John Coltrane can be said to have begun on 23 September 1926. The day on which he was born, as other writers have pointed out, was the autumn equinox—one of the two occasions in the year when night and day enjoy a fleeting equality. The rest of the year, or the rest of one's life, is a different story for, at any moment, either night or day predominates and each individual has to try to maintain an artificial balance between the two or undergo the influence of first one and then the other.

The ambiguities of Coltrane's personality seem to be detectable from his childhood onwards, and they are important for an understanding of his music. An offspring of the black middle-class of the 1920s, he was well cared for, well dressed and almost abnormally well behaved. He acquired early on a kind of reserved intensity in his dealing with others, even with his school colleagues James Kinzer and Franklin Brower. In the words of one of his biographers, Cuthbert Simpkins, 'On the outside John, like his parents, was quiet but inside he burned with the energy of Rev. Blair.'

The Reverend was John's maternal grandfather and the pastor of St. Stephen's African Methodist Episcopal Church in High Point, N. Carolina. Although John William Coltrane was actually born in nearby Hamlet, his mother Alice and his father John Robert Coltrane (J.R. for short) had moved when the baby was very young to live in the house of Rev. and Mrs. Blair. This meant that, not only was there a strong religious influence in John's early life, but he was aware of his grandfather's standing in the black community and his political activities to improve the lot of his parishioners. This may not seem too much of a contradiction today, after Martin Luther King and Jesse Jackson, but it was certainly untypical for the 1920s.

The move meant that John was surrounded by a close-knit family structure, even more so when Alice's sister with her husband and daughter (John's cousin Mary) moved into the same house. This was a set-up that was perhaps restrictive, certainly in terms of privacy, but not as oppressive as it might have been. It provided companionship for the two cousins, who were of similar age (Mary being a year younger) and neither of whom had any brothers or sisters, and it provided security and a base from which to spread one's wings when the time came. Perhaps it was Rev. Blair's involvement beyond the confines of the church which allowed young John to acquire the art of tolerating others' opinions and, later, a genuine intellectual curiosity about other religions. He also allowed son-in-law J.R., far from being pressed into service in the church, to retain his individuality and earn the respect of his own son. And J.R. it was who provided John with his first experiences of non-religious music, playing country-style violin and, equally self-taught, accompanying his singing of popular ballads on the ukulele.

With J.R. working long hours in the tailoring shop run by one of the church elders, it was his mother who had the strongest influence on the growing boy. Having studied music at college, which is where she met J.R., she took a keen pleasure in introducing John to the occasional special concerts put on by the church, consisting either of suitably middle-class European music or soberly-arranged Negro spirituals and gospel songs. Sometimes it was visiting groups and choirs who performed at these recitals, but sometimes the church's own choir gave performances outside of the actual services of worship. And the choir's regular pianist and director was Mrs. Coltrane. Whether, being a trained teacher, she also gave John any formal music instruction, or merely provided musical and moral standards to live up to, has not been clarified. But it may be that, if he showed no interest in the piano in his early years, his tolerant parents did not press the point.

From the age of about 10, however, he would have heard the seemingly very different music which was being widely popularised thanks to the radio. Although the development of big-band jazz had been pioneered a decade earlier by people like Fletcher Henderson and Duke Ellington, it was the commercial breakthrough of young, clean-cut, white instrumentalists that started the teenage dancing craze of the mid-1930s onwards. Even before he was old enough to be interested in meeting and consorting with the opposite sex, John began listening to the performers who accompanied these social rites. Among the many who fronted their own bands, first Benny Goodman, then Artie Shaw and Woody Herman made an enormous impact on the popular music world. The chosen instrument of all three of these bandleaders was the sometimes flowing, sometimes shrill clarinet and, unaware that it was also an effective phallic symbol, John was ready to be impressed by its sheer sound.

So, when one of Rev. Blair's assistants, Rev. Warren Steele, decided to form High Point's very own Community Band, rehearsing once a week at St. Stephen's Church, it was a clarinet that the 12-year-old John most wanted to play. In fact, he had to start on E-flat alto horn, or peck-horn as it is sometimes called, but he joined in with a will and even enjoyed the middle-of-the-road marching-band music that Rev. Steele favoured. By the time he was given the chance to switch over to clarinet, he had learned the basics of reading music and ensemble playing, and expressed his enthusiasm by regular practice at home. It has been suggested that John's father also had some knowledge of the clarinet but, if he had possessed one himself, John would surely have gravitated to it sooner, and it may be that J.R. only showed his interest after his son brought home the church-owned instrument lent him by the band.

Shortly after this welcome acquisition, however, life at home changed radically when John's father died suddenly in 1939 (co-incidentally, the same year in which Charlie Parker too lost his father but with vastly different consequences, given the difference in personality and age between Coltrane and Parker, who was born in 1920). John's mother had not only been very close to him but she had been a constant presence in the extended family that shared Rev. Blair's house. Now, though, she had to find domestic work outside the home in order to support herself and her son while, with the diverging interests of adolescent boys and girls, John and cousin Mary had far less time for each other as well. The net result was that Coltrane not only had more freedom to study his instrument thoroughly, but he began to realise the power of music as a solace and as a means of expressing unspoken feelings. Now the only child was no longer alone, for in music he discovered a companion who would not desert him.

That same year John and his classmates moved up to William Penn High School, where his academic work levelled out to a fairly uninspired average performance good enough to keep him out of trouble, but no more. The high standards he had been encouraged to strive for by the family were all channelled into his music-making, and the first signs of an obsessive devotion to the subject began to surface in his lengthy and open-ended practice sessions, sometimes in the early hours of the morning. John's technical facility was soon much greater than was required for the Community Band and was motivated by a growing interest in the sounds of jazz improvisation. The other contributory factor was the continuing break-up of the family home, as within a year of his father's death both Rev. Blair and cousin Mary's father also died. John and Mary remained, with their grandmother, until their graduation from high school but John's mother, no longer fearing Rev. Blair's disapproval, moved away to Atlantic City to find a better-paying domestic job. Now that his mother's disapproval had in turn been removed, John was socialising more with his peers at school and attending his first teenage parties. As a result, he became more interested in the black music heritage that lay behind the success of the popular white bands, and in the few black organisations that were sufficiently well promoted to be heard on national radio—Ellington, Jimmy Lunceford, Cab Calloway and Count Basie.

John was particularly fond of the first two and learned, by ear, to play on his clarinet the saxophone solo from Lunceford's version of *Margie*. But the early 1940s was an intriguing time to be listening to big-band music, as on the one hand certain trends in the groups just mentioned were leading towards the establishment of a new, more experimental small-band style, which eventually became known as bebop. On the other hand, while the top white bands flirted with pallid arrangements of the piano-blues popularly called 'boogie-woogie', some regionally-based black bands were effecting a much more profound interaction between jazz and blues. Two records which made a considerable impact on John, as well as his contemporaries, were *After Hours* by Erskine Hawkins featuring pianist Avery Parrish—an enormous hit in 1940—and the following year's Earl Hines success *Jelly Jelly* (with Billy Eckstine's vocal referring, probably for the first time outside of 'race records' destined solely for the urban ghettos, to the sexual term 'jelly roll'). In the same year, the Jay McShann band scored with their equally explicit *Confessin' the Blues,* the B-side of which contained the first issued solo of one Charlie Parker. The rhythm-and-blues blend which such records crystallised in the 1940s was to become the major source of employment for a large number of black musicians, Coltrane among them.

Even before he became aware of emerging stylistic trends, however, and certainly before he ever heard of Charlie Parker, John was becoming more interested in the alto saxophone. Performers who took the melodic lead in recordings by Duke Ellington (most frequently the great Johnny Hodges) or by the Lunceford band (where Willie Smith was featured on *Margie* and others) began to appeal more directly than the clarinettists he had first paid attention to. There was none of the piercing quality of the clarinet; even in its upper register the alto had a huge full-bodied sound which, in the hands of the master saxophonists, mirrored the vocal cry of the gospel singers and the bluesmen. It was hardly surprising that, when he learned of a local black restaurant-owner called Charlie Haygood who was a part-time alto player, he sought advice and was rewarded with permission to practice on Haygood's horn. A further incentive to get involved with the saxophone was that the High School in 1942 started its own band under the supervision of the music teacher and, as well as being a featured soloist on clarinet, John started bringing along his borrowed saxophone. He was now benefitting from the learning process of playing with other musicians, even where the music was not the kind he now preferred. And he was beginning to organise little amateur sessions with fellow band members in the basement of his home. When he confided to his mother that these activities were becoming important to him, she put some of her Atlantic City earnings into the purchase of a second-hand alto which would be his very own.

Immediately after he graduated from high school on 31 May 1943, John followed his mother's example and moved North in search of remunerative employment. He went not to Atlantic City but to Philadelphia, which was at least nearer to his mother than he had been living for the last few years. In Philly, his fellow student Franklin Brower had relatives and, while both Franklin and James Kinzer had set their sights on going to college, John started working as a labourer in a sugar factory. Sharing a room with James, he soon saved enough to start regular saxophone lessons at the Ornstein School of Music, virtually his first formal instruction of any kind, since Rev. Steele and his high-school teachers scarcely knew more than how to finger a basic scale. Here he encountered other aspiring jazz players such as Bill Barron and specific saxophone tuition from Mike Guerra, who told biographer J.C. Thomas, 'I wrote out complex chord progressions and special exercises in chromatic scales, and he was one of the few who brought his homework back practically the next day and played it on sight . . . He was always asking for more.' Perhaps his perfectionism reflected a lack of confidence which kept him tied to his private practice and deprived him of the time to make full contact with the many established musicians based in Philadelphia, although entry into the profession was actually easier than it would have been in peacetime and many teenagers in a hurry (such as Stan Getz, who was four months younger than Coltrane) were already full-time professionals on the national big-band scene.

But John was either not in a hurry, or less sure of his direction, and he was eighteen before he joined the musicians' union and began working full-time with the trio in a cocktail lounge. Whether this would have provided a real introduction to the Philadelphia scene is anyone's guess for, now that he was of age to be drafted, his military nemesis caught up with him and he was duly inducted into the navy. Fortunately, his professional status permitted him to be assigned to a band, and he spent the last six months of his tour of duty stationed in Hawaii, playing every day. To be sure, it was marching music again—and clarinet again—but there was also the opportunity to play his saxophone in the unit's dance band, plus a lot of free time in which to listen to the popular music of the day. An indication of what he was hearing on radio and records around this period (and of his ease of recollection many years later) may be gleaned from listing some of the songs he subsequently chose to record, such as Cole Porter's *I Love You* and *Ev'ry Time We Say Goodbye* which were both popular in 1945, as were *Like Someone in Love* and *Out of This World.* The existence of Coltrane versions of both of the songs issued on a single record in 1945, Billy Eckstine's *I Want to Talk About You* and *I'll Wait and Pray* (featuring Sarah Vaughan), may even point to a particular sentimental identification with a so far unnamed girlfriend left behind in Philadelphia.

John Coltrane Photo: David Redfern

On his return in June 1946, John once again went to live with his mother who, although only there at weekends because of the demands of her work, now had a Philadelphia apartment. With her moral support and his demobilisation money, he was determined to concentrate on music and to avoid taking a day job. Resuming his saxophone lessons and constant practising, he gradually became well enough known on the still thriving local scene to be called for out-of-town gigs with the rhythm-and-blues bands of first Joe Webb (whose singer, Maybelle Smith, was later extremely popular as Big Maybelle) and then King Kolax. With the addition of the younger Benny Golson, John and Bill Barron formed an inseparable trio, just like that of John's schooldays with Franklin and James except that the cement of this relationship was the new music on the jazz scene. The regimented polish of the top white bands, so popular during the war, was rapidly undermined in the aftermath of victory, and much more of interest to younger black musicians was the bebop style, which had emerged as a fully-fledged movement. As soon as the first records of bebop had become generally disseminated during John's time in the navy, everyone in his circle was talking about the wildly funny Dizzy Gillespie and the wildly imaginative Charlie Parker. And, especially if you were a saxophonist, the brilliance of Parker posed a challenge it was impossible to ignore. Coltrane himself was to say in later years, 'When I had first heard Bird, I wanted to be identified with him . . . to be consumed by him. But underneath I really wanted to be myself. You can only play so much of another man.'

One of the gigs with King Kolax, which took him as far as Los Angeles, even enabled John to meet his idol. According to Earl Coleman, he attended Bird's *Dark Shadows* record date in February 1947 and went on to a jam session with him afterwards, which must have given Coltrane a lot to think about.

Nevertheless, in working his way through this challenge, John's practising paid off to such an extent that, not only was he undaunted by Parker's amazing technique, he found it easier to understand his approach than many would-be emulators of Bird. Another musician bitten by the bebop bug was Johnny Griffin, two years younger than Coltrane but already touring nationally with Lionel Hampton in 1946-47, and he gave me this first-hand glimpse of the young Coltrane: 'When I had time off in New York City with Elmo Hope and the brother of Jackie Paris the singer, we would go to Philadelphia, stay at 'Philly Joe' Jones's apartment, and go out jamming every night . . . (Coltrane) always had a very precise, intelligent approach to music, plus his own way of playing. But during this inital period he was, I guess like most musicians, very influenced by Dexter Gordon and Sonny Stitt and Bird. The man himself was a formidable musician. I mean, not just playing the saxophone but with his knowledge of music technically.'

This was the Coltrane who, as he later admitted, should have been capitalising on his assets and extending himself musically in the late 1940s. But many obstacles would have to be overcome in the next ten years before Coltrane could feel that he was doing justice to 'his own way of playing'.

Chapter Three

Some time in late 1947, John Coltrane almost made the big-time. That is, he was invited to join his first 'name' band, when singer and saxophonist Eddie 'Cleanhead' Vinson came to Philadelphia without a group of his own and proceeded to form one. A former star sideman with Cootie Williams's orchestra, Vinson had struck out on his own in the mid-40s and became even more successful, with a couple of hit vocal records. He had been given an expensive big-band backing (just like Cootie or Billy Eckstine, or indeed anyone who was making it big during the war), and he had been given a share in an expensive night-club; having lost them both in the change of climate that followed the war, he was making do with smaller, usually 7-piece groups.

Although Cleanhead has belatedly received credit as a pioneer rhythm-and-blues stylist, his blues singing was much more 'down home' than Louis Jordan's, for instance, while his jazz instrumentals (such as *Tune Up* and *Four,* both later recorded by Miles Davis) were strongly influenced by bebop. It was the vocals which sold the records but Vinson was still a jazzman at heart, and as a result he made a habit of hiring jazz musicians to play with him. As he told me, 'I had this group with [pianist] Red Garland, Johnny Coltrane and [trumpeter] Johnny Coles, but what we played was a little too advanced for the people. We would play warehouses and big halls down in the Carolinas, and Georgias and Alabamas, where they wasn't really hip to jazz, you know. And they wanted to hear the blues. But, if the gig started at 9, we would start at 8 and, by the time the people got in, we were still playing. And, when they'd gone, we'd wait till they get out and play after, till the bus is loaded up. And then we'd get out to the next town.'

This split-personality band must have been ultimately unsatisfying for someone as fascinated by bebop as Coltrane. (Incidentally, Vinson claims that John never recorded with his band, while Coltrane himself described as his record 'debut' the much later occasion on which he cut his first solo; the four tracks reissued on Vinson's Saxophonograph LP have solos which are probably the work of one Red Carman). But the liaison had important consequences since Cleanhead, being an alto saxist himself, obliged John to fill out the group sound by taking up the tenor. Despite associating with tenor players such as Bill Barron and Benny Golson, he had never been drawn to the larger instrument, but by now it had become a case of 'no tenor, no job'. John needed both the money and the experience and, though he stayed for rather less than a year, it is clear that he began to pay closer attention to the illustrious forebears on his newly acquired horn: Lester Young, who was then enjoying his greatest popularity, and—perhaps more important still for John in the long run—Coleman Hawkins and Don Byas.

Back in Philadelphia, however, he reverted to what he still considered his main instrument, the alto (his only extended improvisations on alto, though, date from a 1958 session with Gene Ammons, and give little idea of how he must have sounded in 1948). By and large, he found the work situation was far from ideal, thanks to a general economic recession. Locally-based rhythm-and-blues groups were happy to employ the former Cleanhead sideman, but only at the local union rates, and John was aware that they were setting their sights far lower than Vinson. Already by the late 40s, John was known locally as 'The Train', doubtless because of his surging solo style and particularly his unswerving devotion to jazz. But the only musical stimulus during this period came from his friendships with a young trumpeter and composer born in Philadelphia but brought up in Pittsburgh, Calvin Massey, and with the saxophone playing member of Philly's famous Heath Brothers. Jimmy Heath, just one month younger than Coltrane, told interviewer Russell Davies, 'We practised together. We went with girlfriends, we dated together, in other words. We went to the Philadelphia Library and did a lot of research on classical music, listening to Stravinsky and other people. And we transcribed things from records, and analysed what Charlie Parker and the other people were doing before our time, Lester Young and others.'

Heath was very involved in the compositional aspects of bebop, as well as being an excellent Parker-inspired alto player, known far and wide as 'Little Bird'. In 1948 he had gone so far as to form an enterprising big-band, featuring John and himself on altos and Johnny Coles and Cal Massey on trumpets, among others. This band, which never recorded, was sufficiently promising for Parker's former trumpeter Howard McGhee, who had previously employed Jimmy and Percy Heath in his sextet, to adopt it en masse as his backing band for a few engagements including one at the famous Apollo Theatre in Harlem. But, in its home town, the band played more often for kicks than for payment, and even the latter occasions were small neighbourhood events for the more jazz-minded members of the black community. A highlight was undoubtedly the occasion on which they provided the backing for none other than Charlie Parker himself, doing a one-off appearance as guest soloist, but on the whole it was just as well that the band members valued the experience more than the remuneration.

As the 1940s drew to a close, it was becoming evident that, while bebop had acquired a small hard-core audience of dedicated fans, even the black population had not exactly taken it to their hearts. The mainstream music industry had shown some brief interest, and attempted to build up the winning personality of Dizzy Gillespie into the base for a commodity that could become marketable, no matter who the performers were. But the performers, even Gillespie himself, and certainly the general public, proved too resistant to this ploy, while the industry went back to exploiting other minority musics such as Latin-American, hillbilly and even calypso. So, once again, it was the big-time-but-not-quite when in late 1949 Gillespie hired the nucleus of the Philadelphia boppers as replacements in his big-band, including both John and Jimmy Heath, drummer Specs Wright, pianist John Acea and trombonist Charles Greenlee (Muslim name: Harnifan Majid), who subsequently married John's cousin Mary.

The repertoire that Dizzy was using in concert was still absorbing and challenging—at least part of it was, such as Tadd Dameron's *Soulphony* and Thelonious Monk's *'Round Midnight,* on which Coltrane was featured (both of these arrangements can be heard on earlier live

John Coltrane (r) with Tommy Potter, Charlie Parker and Dizzy Gillespie at Birdland, New York, in 1951
Photo: Frank Driggs Collection

recordings with John's predecessors). But the material on Gillespie's official record sessions of the period had already begun emphasising the comedy vocals, especially after Dizzy had to change record labels in 1949; and of course the live performances increasingly reflected the need to publicise the records. Nevertheless, in terms of John's dedication to improvised jazz and his still somewhat undefined aims for the future, this was by far the most prestigious job he had held down to date, and it lasted for a year. It was probably when Gillespie had to fold the big-band through lack of sufficient engagements that John played a couple of gigs at the Audubon Ballroom on New York's 166th St. with such people as Sonny Rollins, Bud Powell and Art Blakey; and there was at least one session with Miles Davis leading both Rollins and Coltrane.

Fortunately, John then switched once again to tenor saxophone in order to join Dizzy's new small-group which initially included Jimmy Heath too, although pretty soon Heath was dropped and John was the only saxophonist in the group. The surviving broadcasts by this sextet provide the first documentation of the then 24-year-old Coltrane, just as he was beginning finally to acclimatise himself to the horn he was to be identified with for the next decade. It is documentation that is all the more valuable since the one studio session he made with Dizzy at the time was also the first-ever for Gillespie's own record company (a sign of the hard times which had befallen bebop); the commercial logistics of trying to establish Dee Gee Records allowed John no solo space at all on the two new instrumentals featuring Dizzy himself, and only 20 bars on a rhythm-and-blues vocal number, *We Love To Boogie*. But the air-shots from Birdland show John sounding already quite recognisable while still in the throes of stylistic uncertainties. His fluency on the tenor is not in question and his tone is capable of interesting and original inflections, but the phraseology is a slightly uncomfortable mixture. There is quite a bit of straightforward Lester Young (including, on *Congo Blues*, a direct quotation in homage) together with strong suggestions of Dexter Gordon's boppish edge. (The similarity is so marked at times that an album containing one of these broadcasts actually credits the tenor work to Dexter!) As an indication of things to come, there are the occasional hints of non-Western scales in minor-key numbers such as *Birks' Works* and particularly the saxophone break of *Night In Tunisia*.

While he was working with the Gillespie small-group, Coltrane was getting a reasonable amount of solo space and extending himself in public more than was previously possible, no doubt aided by such inspiring rhythm-section men as Percy Heath and, at least while the band was based in New York, Billy Taylor and Art Blakey. Consequently, he was learning more about himself, and not only musically; he once said to Kitty Grime, 'I don't make a habit of wishing for what I don't have, but I often wish I had a lighter nature. Dizzy has that beautiful gift—I can't say, be happy, people, it's something I can't command. But you have to be true to your own nature.'

Unfortunately for him, the job came to an end, and John found himself back in Philadelphia studying the tenor saxophone this time, and especially its long tradition. As he said later, 'There's a whole lot back there that all young musicians should hear.' But the immediate prospects for employment were unpromising. As trumpeter Ted Curson, then finishing high-school with the youngest of the Heath family, drummer Albert, explained to me, 'A lot of people on the way to New York, or sort of being shoved out of New York for a moment, landed in Philadelphia. That's why we had so many great artists there. Not because there were jobs, there were no jobs.' For jazz, in fact, the early 1950s was a fairly bleak period unless you were a white West Coast musician, and the only work available to Coltrane was in noisy neighbourhood bars where the rhythm-and-blues had to be even noisier than the customers, and a honking and wailing tenor player had to carry most of the responsibility for pleasing the crowd.

There are two different estimates of when Coltrane started using hard drugs, both of them extremely vague. If musical frustrations are thought of as the main reason, he had his share of these throughout the second half of the 1940s and, already during his stint with 'Cleanhead' Vinson, he was drinking quite heavily. In addition, he had and continued to have severe problems with his teeth—which is not exactly good news for a saxophonist. As to the more general frustration of the black population during this period when the increased social expectations aroused by the war years had been rapidly snuffed out, this was neatly paralleled by the hopes of young musicians involved in the creation of bebop and its subsequent rejection. When you consider that the profound desire for an escape of some kind was matched by the efforts of organised crime to increase drug sales in the ghetto areas (plus the all-too-symbolic fact that Charlie Parker, the most instinctively brilliant musician of his generation, was one of the first to become hooked), you have an almost inevitable scenario.

Certainly it would have been difficult to be a member of the Gillespie big-band, or indeed any bop-oriented group big or small, without associating with users and addicts. It seems likely that Coltrane's habit dated from the late 40s, and indeed there were many players who became involved then but only fell foul of the law in the 50s, Jimmy Heath and Howard McGhee among them. It is perhaps fortunate that, not yet being a well-known name in the music business and not being based in New York City, John was not of interest to the narcotics officials there, and undoubtedly his strong religious background deterred him from the kind of anti-social acts which would bring him to the attention of law-enforcement authorities. Indeed, unlike most other users, his motives for investigating drugs in the first place may have been more in the nature of a search for transcendental spiritual experience, for the beginnings of his interest in non-Western religions also date from this time. But, equally, all the pains and problems of becoming addicted to illegal substances were to be, for the next several years, turned inwards on himself.

It was perhaps a year after he left Gillespie that Coltrane's reputation as an efficient, if reluctant, rhythm-and-blues honker in such local bands as Lonnie Slappy's landed him a position with the singer/saxophonist Gay Crosse. From there, it was a significant step to join the touring group of altoist Earl Bostic. Bostic did not sing, but his records sold (in enormous quantities for the period) because of the leader's raucous and oversimplified jazzing-up of melodies such as *Flamingo* and *Temptation*. Thus, while the band's live work for dancers might have allowed equal time for the other musicians, on the eight tunes they recorded while Coltrane was a member he and the other horns usually play just the final chord! Bostic, however, was a veteran of the Don Redman and Lionel Hampton bands and a highly skilled saxophonist, expert in tonal manipulation and in reaching the high harmonics beyond the instrument's normal range. John took the opportunity of consulting Bostic about these matters which were to bear fruit in his own later work, fortunately losing no time about it since he only held the job for nine months or less.

Then it was back to his mother's place in Philadelphia, and back to

John Coltrane on tenor sax Photo: Impulse Records

the local bar bands such as the immortal Daisy Mae and the Hepcats. Not only were these far less well paid than the Bostic group, but their lack of musical interest undoubtedly helped Coltrane to become far less reliable professionally. However, as well as the bad teeth and the drugs that were now with him all the time, it was a period of constant practice and constant study which John hoped would eventually bring about a breakthrough to something new. What that might be he didn't know, but in the meantime he was beginning to listen to non-Western music and to learn all manner of exotic scales. Simultaneously he was studying recorded jazz in depth and familiarising himself with basic jazz phraseology in all the twelve keys. For instance Jimmy Heath, who had by now also switched to tenor sax, recalled that 'D-flat was the most robust and heavy key for the tenor, and all the older tenor players played in D-flat. A lot of the younger players would try to stay away from it 'cos it was quite difficult . . . (John) developed playing in D-flat to the same facility that (he had) in the key of C.'

One of the older players, of the alto saxophone persuasion but nevertheless fond of the key of D-flat, was the next bandleader who took Coltrane on the road, in late 1953, once again around a year after his previous touring job had come to an end. Former Ellington star Johnny Hodges, John's hero of a decade earlier, was then leading his own small group and having some success in appealing to the same audience as Earl Bostic, although with superior jazz improvisation. Once again and for the same reason, the studio recordings on which Coltrane is present have no solo work from him, but there is a fascinating document of the band playing a dance gig that brings us up to date on his development. Although the Al Sears role on Hodges's R-and-B hit *Castle Rock* affords the only chance on record to hear Coltrane doing the honking routine—and doing it well—his three other solo contributions suggest an attempt to apply the astringent tone of Dexter Gordon to the convoluted ideas of Don Byas. There is even an example of his obsessive practising as, immediately after *In A Mellotone,* he repeatedly runs over a couple of fast phrases between numbers! Overall there is a marked increase in the authority of his playing, particularly of his strikingly economical ballad feature in the jukebox style of Gene Ammons or Sonny Stitt, *Don't Blame Me.*

Hodges, of course, was a master of the saxophone ballad and, by his own admission, Coltrane learned much from studying his superb control of tone and line. But, whatever the reasons for John's departure from the Gillespie and Bostic bands, this time it was definitely the unreliability caused by his alternate drinking and drug-taking that terminated his stay with Hodges, again after only nine months or so. On his return to Philly to get straightened out, his reputation curtailed his employability even on the local scene. Ted Curson remembered him being at a loose end musically in late 1954: 'I always admired his playing and he used to write out little things for me, you know, the blues changes and stuff. But he never had a job, and one New Year's Eve—New Year's Eve, people work when they never worked the whole year!—well, he had no job. So I took him on my job, and he played *Nancy With The Laughing Face*, I'll never forget that. I never heard anything so great, so intense, with so much feeling.'

Chapter Four

At this mid-point of the 1950s, Coltrane's career seemed to be going nowhere in particular. Apart from his bandleaders and their associates, and some Philadelphia musicians such as conga player Bill Carney and organist Jimmy Smith with whom he worked in 1955, he had not made much of an impression on anyone. There were still only 20 bars of his solo work on disc, and in any case Dee Gee Records were now unavailable and the company bankrupt. Yet he was already 28, an age by which all of his most famous predecessors had already made a nationwide impact on at least their fellow performers: Louis Armstrong, Coleman Hawkins, Art Tatum, Lester Young, Dizzy Gillespie, Charlie Parker, Miles Davis . . .

Miles, in fact, was less than four months older than Coltrane, but he had moved to New York at the age of eighteen and, within weeks, had started playing with Parker. Miles it was who now changed the public visibility of Trane (as his nickname came to be spelled) once and for all. At first, though, it hardly seemed like it for, until the autumn of 1955, Miles was not working very often and, when a saxophonist was called for, he had usually used Sonny Rollins. Where he was allowed to bring only one sideman of his own choice to play with local musicians around the country, he always chose drummer 'Philly Joe' Jones. So, when Miles's sudden success at the 1955 Newport Festival made it desirable to form a regular quintet, he hired Jones and fellow Philadelphia resident, pianist Red Garland; and, because Rollins had retired to Chicago to nurse a drug problem and felt unready to make a comeback, Miles took Joe and Red's insistent advice and employed the unknown John Coltrane. As Ted Curson recalled, 'The critics just went crazy, for they just could not understand why he would do such a stupid thing. This was when Sonny Stitt was red-hot, and then Bird had died and they thought that Sonny Stitt would take the throne.'

The quintet, completed by equally unknown Detroit bassist Paul Chambers, began a heavy schedule of recordings (although some of them took years to be released) and club engagements. Club audiences, however, were not yet ready for Miles's fundamental reappraisal of bebop, far more radical than the contemporary Max Roach/Clifford Brown group's approach, and they were particularly unhappy about Philly Joe's overbearing volume and about Coltrane's forays in search of a style. A typical audience member during Miles's visit to the West Coast in early 1956 was pianist Sy Johnson, who remembered that only Miles and Philly Joe showed up for the first night; although Los Angeles-based pianist Sonny Clark and bassist Leroy Vinnegar were rounded up to help out, Miles eventually ordered them to be silent and proceeded to play an entire set with just trumpet and drums. Then, on the second night, listeners had to cope with the extremely spacey rhythm-section sound of the full quintet and its even more unorthodox tenor-player: 'No one had heard of these guys. The music was fantastic, except that nobody could stand Coltrane. He was having trouble with his reed, and everything sounded wrong.'

This reaction is no more negative than most people's at the time, and yet listening to the group's recordings with hindsight causes only surprise that the bafflement was so great. Certainly, one factor may be that, because Coltrane's performance was exploratory rather than reduced to a routine, it was distinctly variable from night to night, and his continued involvement with drugs and heavy drinking would no doubt have accentuated this. Interestingly, unlike the poised-sounding 'Round About Midnight' album, two of the sessions done by the quintet for the Prestige label were recorded as if 'live', with no new material and no retakes, and thus Trane's variability comes across markedly on the four resultant albums ('Cookin'', 'Relaxin'', 'Workin'' and 'Steamin''). It is not that the tenor-player is under the weather but, on adjacent numbers or even during the same solo, he can change from directionless faltering to articulate passion; and all within a style which still leans heavily on Dexter Gordon and perhaps on Sonny Rollins also, but seems to be aiming fitfully for the glittering precision of Parker or even of a pianist like Tatum or Bud Powell.

In retrospect, the quintet was *the* trend-setting group of the second half of the 1950s and, Coltrane's contributions apart, it was easily the most widely imitated. Other more dramatically innovative efforts such as those of Mingus or Cecil Taylor reached only a fraction of Miles's audience at the time, although their paths were made smoother by Miles's simplification and extension of recent bebop practices. The repertoire he chose for the group alternated between demolitions of bop classics such as *Woody'n you, Salt peanuts* and *Well you needn't* and more oblique assaults on standard songs, both of which appealed strongly to Coltrane; and what the laissez-faire Davis set-up afforded him, more than ever before, was the freedom to experiment. As Trane himself said, 'I always felt I wanted to play with Miles. He really put me to work. All the things I started to do in 1955, when I went with him, were some of the things I felt I should have done in '47-'48.' And, although the taciturn Miles would not have said directly to Coltrane what he was saying to the critics ('You know, my tenor-player is the greatest thing since Bird'), Trane would certainly have been aware of Miles's encouragement and approval.

It must have been a shock and a financial blow when Miles broke up the group in order to undertake a European tour as a soloist in November 1956. The more so as, in the same week that he had joined Davis thirteen months earlier, John had married the former Juanita Austin (nee Grubbs) who, with her then five-year-old daughter Antonia, had moved in with his mother in Philadelphia. (On two separate recording sessions around this period, Coltrane gave titles to his original compositions based on the abbreviations of these names, *Nita* and *Toni's Dance* (the latter actually issued as *Slowtrane*), while two other pieces probably written in 1957 but recorded in 1959 used their Muslim names, respectively *Naima* and *Syeeda's Song Flute*.) John had been scrupulous about sending money home regularly and had been resorting to alcohol in order to steer clear of narcotics, but the disappearance of his regular gig was chastening. There were some further dates with Miles on his return, although the fact that on some appearances at New York's Café Bohemia he used both Coltrane and Sonny Rollins was taken by John as a sign that he could not be sure of anything. Miles then disbanded again in March 1957 in order to spend a couple of months collaborating with Gil Evans on the album 'Miles Ahead.'

John returned, discouraged, to Philadelphia and began working with local musicians, including the crippled trumpeter Johnny Splawn (a friend of Clifford Brown and influence on Lee Morgan) and the 17-year-old pianist McCoy Tyner. He was dissatisfied with himself for not having made more conclusive use of the opportunities given to him by Miles, now seemingly at an end. He was also becoming disgusted with his dependancy on stimulants of one kind or another, and gradually making up his mind—like Miles himself some three years earlier—to straighten out once and for all. Another factor which urged him in this direction may well have been that the Prestige company, who had lost Miles to Columbia Records in 1956, were astutely offering to put Coltrane himself under contract—and Trane would no doubt have been aware that certain record-labels with the right connections were more than happy to pay their artists in hard drugs rather than hard cash. John was finally impelled to take a self-imposed cure 'cold turkey', with only the encouragement and moral support of his Christian mother and his Muslim wife.

Once again there is conflicting evidence about the date of this event. It may have taken place some months after the start of Coltrane's Prestige contract, but on balance it seems most likely to have been in early 1957. Certainly at this time, during his last stay of any length in Philadelphia, he began to throw himself more and more into his music, and one aspect of his experimentation began to fall into place.

According to McCoy Tyner, the material later recorded on the album 'Giant Steps', plus other trend-setting items such as *Like Sonny* and *Equinox*, were all composed and rehearsed with himself and other local musicians at this period: 'I used to go over to his mother's house, when he was working on those cycles, you know. And, actually, I knew those songs before they recorded them, but I was still in Philadelphia so he used Tommy Flanagan on the album.' Tyner also told me that the unique harmonic plan of *Giant Steps* itself (discussed further in Chapter 7) was apparently inspired by the closing bars of an Art Tatum record, probably his 1953 version of *Have You Met Miss Jones?* Interestingly, the first non-Coltrane recording of *Giant Steps* was done, by pianist Jaki Byard, in an Art Tatum style. Either way, as Tyner said, 'A lot of things may appear to be minute, but you can sometimes utilise them on a larger scale', which is certainly true of what Coltrane created with *Giant Steps*.

While still residing in Philadelphia and making only the occasional trip to New York for recording, Coltrane received an invitation to join Thelonious Monk, first of all for guest appearances on two record sessions. And then, in the summer, he became for sixteen weeks a member of the quartet (with bassist Wilbur Ware and first 'Philly Joe' Jones, then Shadow Wilson, on drums) for what was virtually Monk's first-ever New York nightclub residency, at the old Five Spot. For the fortunate few who heard it, including Coltrane's later colleague Elvin Jones, and McCoy Tyner who made the pilgrimage from Philadelphia specially to listen to the group, Monk's quartet had even more of an impact than the Miles Davis quintet. Regrettably, perhaps, it had far less influence because, despite the rumours of hours of private recordings from the Five Spot in the possession of Naima, all that was ever heard beyond the doors of the club itself consisted of three tracks recorded around a year later, and not released until 1961 (this was apparently because, although Prestige would have allowed Coltrane to appear again on Monk's record label of that time, Monk was bitter about his own earlier experiences with Prestige and would not agree to any negotiations with them).

It is clear, however, from his other recordings of the period that, now that Trane had reformed himself, he was able to be simultaneously exploratory and fluent, rather than either one or the other; and he found it enormously stimulating to thread his way through Monk's intricate yet spare designs, making explicit what had been implicit, with vast outpourings of notes unlike anything previously heard on the saxophone. Now the influence of Dexter Gordon had more or less disappeared, and instead the relentless harmonic thrusts of Hawkins, Don Byas and possibly Byas disciple Paul Gonsalves (with whom Trane had played in the Gillespie big band) provided the key. But it was Coltrane who opened the door for a new style of tenor playing, aptly described as 'sheets of sound', in which ideally the performer would never have to breathe between phrases and would never be at a loss for permutations of scales and arpeggios, whatever the chord sequence.

Trane was now very much in demand for record sessions, making a total of twelve albums under his own name during 1957-58, eleven of

Miles Davies

them resulting from his two-year contract with Prestige, although their release was carefully spread over the next several years. Most of these were recorded in the no-rehearsal no-retake studio style that Prestige had actually learned from Miles Davis, whereas 'Blue Train' (on Blue Note Records) had a more prepared feel about it. One Prestige session, which produced enough material for an album and two halves of albums, was notable for the inclusion of pieces by McCoy Tyner (*The Believer,* in waltz time) and by Cal Massey

(*Nakatini Serenade*); other absorbing compositions were introduced into Coltrane's first two quartet albums, namely *Slow Dance* (by Alonzo Levister) and *Theme For Ernie,* written by Philadelphia guitarist Fred Lacey in memory of the recently deceased Ernie Henry. On all of these recordings, Trane himself is far more consistently creative than on his 1955-56 dates with Miles, and this applies equally to no fewer than 28 studio albums as a sideman from this period (many of which were actually marketed with his name prominently featured, or actually released or re-released as 'Coltrane albums'). In this way, Trane worked with everyone from Cecil Taylor to George Russell to Michel Legrand, all of whom spoke enthusiastically about his work. Taylor, who had admired Coltrane but never played with him before, remembered that 'He was involved in trying to find out just what there was in the piano music that he could relate to . . . The thing I dug about Trane was that with him it was a matter of music, it was never a matter of personality. Music was all he was concerned with.'

The factor which crowned Coltrane's growing authority and widening acceptance, firstly by musicians and finally by listeners, was rejoining Miles Davis in 1958. His new quintet already included altoist Cannonball Adderley, and for a while Red Garland and 'Philly Joe' Jones returned, to be soon replaced by Bill Evans and Jimmy Cobb. The addition of Coltrane created a three-piece frontline but, unlike the comparable line-up arranged by Benny Golson for the Jazztet starting in 1959 or that of the Jazz Messengers from 1961 onwards, there seemed to be even less ensemble work than in Miles's earlier quintet. The impression given was that it was every man for himself, except for the briefest introductions and endings—a deceptive impression, because Miles was working on quite new ways of creating a group identity, through performances based on the sparsest kind of modal material. And, although this approach turned out to be ideally suited to Coltrane and he has been credited with playing a large part in creating the approach, it is clear that Miles was the instigator. Trane himself said as much when he noted that 'I found Miles in the midst of another stage of his musical development . . . Now it seemed that he was moving . . . to the use of fewer and fewer chord changes in songs. He used tunes with free-flowing lines and chordal direction. This approach allowed the soloist the choice of playing chordally (vertically) or melodically (horizontally).'

And yet, some of the 1955-56 Miles quintet performances of more standard material sound almost like rehearsals for this concept, even though it had yet to be articulated. The recording of *Dear Old Stockholm* (in which Trane casually demonstrated his familiarity with Davis's 1952 version) can be heard as a sort of pre-echo of the sextet number *So what,* just as the bouncy *Ah-leu-cha,* except for the theme itself, foreshadows the title track of 'Milestones'. But what especially marked the in-person performances of the sextet, as confirmed by live recordings issued subsequently, was the seemingly disproportionate length of Coltrane's solos. Numerous anecdotes have been told of Miles's tolerant but somewhat bemused attitude to this aspect of the tenorist's work, and Jimmy Heath has recounted Trane's response to being questioned about it: '"I couldn't find nothing good to stop on"—he meant musically—so Miles said "All you gotta do is take the horn out of your mouth".' Drummer Art Taylor, who worked on many of Coltrane's recording sessions of this period and briefly in public on an engagement by the Red Garland quintet (before both men rejoined Davis), told Russell Davies how his practising at home reflected this constant search for musical perfection. Trane had by now moved his family to New York, but 'I'd come in the house and he'd be practising, so I'd sit there and I would talk with (Naima) for hours. So I'd know her better than I know him. 'Cause she would never disturb him, and I would sit there two or three hours sometimes, he'd just keep on practising.'

Each of the two-and-a-half studio albums made by this Davis group has its own kind of intensity, that of 'Milestones' being accentuated by the fact that four out of five sextet tracks have no piano or bass solos; the fifth, the slightly more serene medium-tempo *Straight No Chaser* has a stunning solo by Coltrane which, as with several other solos of this period, contrasts basic blues phrases at the start of a chorus with fantastically involved Traneries for the remainder of the 12 bars. The standard songs of the 'Jazz Track' album, on the other hand, have a delicacy that conceals hidden passions, especially Coltrane's almost straight melody-playing on *Stella By Starlight* and his jaunty sound in *On Green Dolphin Street;* the latter may well have been suggested to Miles by Trane, since he recorded two similar film themes by the same composer (Bronislau Kaper), *Invitation* and *While My Lady Sleeps* (the opening phrase of which was at this period by far his favourite quotation during improvisations on other tunes). And finally, of course, 'Kind Of Blue' moves even further from the conventional modern jazz of the day towards a sort of spiritual awe depicted in music.

One or other of these records won over most of the remaining detractors of Coltrane himself and, taken together wth Miles's next project with Gil Evans ('Sketches Of Spain'), they prepared the audience of the coming decade for the sounds of musicians as different as Ornette Coleman and Ravi Shankar—and, of course, for the John Coltrane quartet.

Chapter Five

During the last months with Miles Davis, Coltrane had already begun to expand his musical interests more than ever before. The music of Ravi Shankar was something which he became aware of at this period, as he did the very different culture being drawn on by US-based African drummer Michael Olatunji (later to be honoured in a Coltrane tune-title, *Tunji*). And, perhaps especially relevant to his subsequent work, he began to be attracted by the 'Moorish' sound of certain kinds of Arabic music, initially as filtered through other American instrumentalists. He said in 1960, 'I like Eastern music; Yusef Lateef has been using this in his playing for some time. And Ornette Coleman sometimes plays music with a Spanish content as well as other exotic-flavoured music. In these approaches there's something I can draw on and use in the way I play.' The pages of his notebook reproduced in Simpkins's biography show at one point a series of eighteen different non-diatonic scales, including Chinese, Japanese, Arabian and Persian examples, as well as a list of the ancient Greek modes. Incidentally, another page illustrates his quiet sense of humour with a reference to '*I Got Rhythm* (approx. 15th century)'.

In the meantime, he had begun to stretch his wings with the occasional gig under his own leadership, including one with a line-up of Elvin Jones, George Tucker on bass, both Tommy Flanagan and Cedar Walton alternating on piano, Freddie Hubbard, and fellow saxophonist Wayne Shorter. Also, his new two-year recording contract with the Atlantic label enabled him to present to the public the

'Giant Steps' material. Thanks to a somewhat increased budget and consequently greater care and attention, Trane was allowed to have more than one try at recording many of these tunes, and indeed to wait eight months before finally approving a version of *Naima* to complete his first Atlantic album. Changes in the rhythm-section personnel from one session to another—it was the third different line-up which achieved the originally issued take of *Naima*—might seem to indicate that they caused the major problems but, if they were in any difficulty, it was because of the challenging and unconventional nature of some of the compositions. Coltrane's own performance, however, probably bothered him more, and the ruthless perfectionism that lay behind his continual practising now surfaced in the studio; the first attempt at *Giant Steps* itself, issued several years after Trane's death, would surely have been perfectly acceptable to anyone less self-critical.

For the first time, he had produced an album entirely consisting of original numbers, which few other performers had done up to this point (only Duke Ellington, Mingus, Sun Ra and Ornette spring to mind). The material covers the gamut from complex chord-sequences to the straight-ahead blues of *Mr. P.C.* (which sounds as if it could easily be a Dexter Gordon line) and *Cousin Mary*. But everything is played with unstoppable drive and a yearning, desolate tone, even at high speed. The second Atlantic album, 'Coltrane Jazz', is arguably more relaxed and more varied, containing as it does three standard songs and an original variation on *What Is This Thing Called Love?* entitled *Fifth House* (a reference both to the astrological domain of love and to Tadd Dameron's *Hot House*). One element of tonal variety is that the closing notes of *I'll Wait And Pray* and much of the theme statement of *Harmonique* features the production of more than one note simultaneously by carefully controlled overblowing, a technique first recorded on the final chord of the 1957 *While My Lady Sleeps*.

Although 'Coltrane Jazz' was the last planned recording with John's colleagues from the Miles Davis band, now including Wynton Kelly on piano, a live album taped in Holland during Miles's spring 1960 tour—which Coltrane had agreed to do after having officially resigned from the group—suggests the reasons for the very mixed reaction of European audiences to their first direct experience of the tenor player. In short, his intensity of tone and multiplicity of notes seem too far removed from the restraint of Miles (and from the elation of the rhythm-section) to form a viable contrast any longer, and there was already a suggestion of this as far back as the 1958 'Jazz At The Plaza' live session, where on *If I Were A Bell* Trane played with more sheer, unrelieved rapidity than perhaps anywhere else on record. Surprisingly, however, there was a sequel when Coltrane made a guest appearance on two rather more subdued 1961 Miles tracks; Jimmy Cobb informed Davis's biographer Ian Carr that Trane entered the studio actually during the performance of *Some Day My Prince Will Come* and joined in, despite never having played the tune before—to such good effect that the opening melody of his classic solo became the source of at least two 'original' compositions, Charles Lloyd's *Love Song To A Baby* and Chick Corea's *La Fiesta*.

The autumn of 1959 when 'Coltrane Jazz' was recorded also saw Coltrane moving his family into a house in the borough of Queens and, when it became clear that he was now more than ready to have a group of his own, Miles encouraged him to sign up with his own manager, Harold Lovett, and with the same booking agency he used, Shaw Artists. Although Trane's first appearance under this new arrangement was with the already constituted Mal Waldron Trio, he soon set about forming a rhythm-section of his own choice. The first pianist in the quartet was the young Steve Kuhn and, although fellow Philadelphian Bobby Timmons was rumoured to be a candidate, it was McCoy Tyner who, although by then away on tour with Benny Golson, soon came in to replace Kuhn. On bass was Steve Davis, also from Philly and at whose house John had first met Naima, while Pete LaRoca was the original drummer. After a few months he made way for Billy Higgins, until Coltrane decided to call on Elvin Jones. 'When John worked for a while with Monk, we got to be very close friends,' Elvin told me. 'And he asked if he did decide to get a group, if I would be interested in working with him. And I told him, of course, yes I would. Then it just happened that, at the time when he actually formed his group, I was working with another band (Harry Edison) so later on, after six months or so, he sent word that he really needed me.' In fact, when Elvin arrived to fill this need, a unique duo was formed, comparable only to that of Charlie Parker and Max Roach, and it became the centrifugal force of Coltrane's group for the next five years.

By autumn 1960 when Elvin joined him, Coltrane had fallen

behind in his recording commitments for Atlantic. He had taken part in, but was not ready to release, a session with Ornette Coleman's sidemen playing a programme of Coleman compositions, which incidentally marked Trane's debut on soprano saxophone. But, now that his rhythm-section had come together, he made up for lost time by recording (Miles Davis-style) nineteen tunes in three days, some of them in more than one take, plus two numbers for just the rhythm trio which he hoped to include as a change of pace like those of the Red Garland Trio on Davis's 'Milestones' and 'Workin'' albums. The results incorporate other changes of texture, with McCoy Tyner dropping out altogether from time to time and Coltrane himself soloing on soprano, usually reserving it for specific numbers although on *26-2* (based on Charlie Parker's *Confirmation*) he uses both tenor and soprano.

In addition the material, which eventually constituted three albums and two further part-albums, embraces a variety of moods which is impressive indeed considering the hypnotic simplicity of many of the pieces, most of which on the surface mark a definitive move away from the *Giant Steps* approach. Much of the repertoire had been worked up in public before being recorded but, according to Tyner, 'There were several occasions where a lot of things were actually made up in the studio, but we played so well together, it was a very tight-knit unit . . . Sometimes (John) would bring in a scale of 8, 9 or 12 notes or whatever, and we would actually create a composition. In the studio, or even if he'd bring it to work (i.e. in a nightclub).' One interesting feature, not unrelated to a 1960 engagement at Small's Paradise which was in Harlem, is the fact that no fewer than eight of the pieces recorded at this period were simple 12-bar blues, though sometimes with non-traditional chord sequences and sometimes in such challenging keys as B and F-sharp. As Tyner said, 'That's what is unique about this music—that sometimes if you really listen to it, you can hear that it actually was an outgrowth from previous music.'

Coltrane's researches into the soprano saxophone were initially sparked off by the death in 1959 of the great Sidney Bechet, and bore unexpected fruit in the recording of Rodgers and Hammerstein's hit song from *The Sound Of Music,* the fast waltz called *My Favourite Things*. Released, like *Naima* before it, as a 45 rpm single this became Trane's most popular number by far, and almost the last time that a

John Coltrane with Cannonball Adderley, Miles Davis and Bill Evans, New York 1958
Photo: Frank Driggs Collection

jazz musician gained commercial success with a Broadway show-tune. With its ¾ beat lending itself to Afro-Cuban-influenced cross-rhythms between Trane and Elvin, and its pedal-point harmonies that led so easily to modal improvisation, it had the added advantage of being in many ways absolutely typical of the quartet's approach, rather than one of those 'accidental' hits that becomes a millstone for the performer concerned. As a result, he was able to gain new inspiration from it night after night, and to play longer and longer solos without feeling that his invention was exhausted. Not that his audiences invariably agreed; and there was also the fact that, if Philly Joe had seemed loud a few years earlier, the volume produced by Elvin when he and Coltrane took off together was just too much for some. Criticism was heard too to the effect that Trane sometimes appeared to neglect his main horn for what many fellow musicians considered 'a minor instrument', although there were ultimately even more younger musicians who were utterly captivated by this 'new sound', sometimes to their own detriment. Writer Richard Williams once noted, in a radio discussion of Coltrane, how these disciples soon found that, on the soprano, 'It's easier to sound convincing. It's easier to make that kind of vaguely ululating Indian sound, that tends to lull people into trances.'

If the introduction of the soprano into the quartet was a sign of Trane's concern for texture, it was not the only one for, shortly after these recordings, Steve Davis was replaced by Reggie Workman (also from Philadelphia); but the latter was often augmented on records and some live dates, first by Art Davis and then by Jimmy Garrison, who took over as the regular bassist from the end of 1961. And, for the live recording at the Village Vanguard in November 1961, some of the originally unissued tracks involved the veteran reedman Garvin Bushell and the former Monk bassist Ahmed Abdul-Malik playing an oriental-sounding drone on the bassoon and the Middle-Eastern *oud* respectively. More significantly for the immediate development of the group, Coltrane had been thinking about the addition of more improvising soloists and, as early as the September 1960 trip to San Francisco's Jazz Workshop and the Monterey Festival, both guitarist Wes Montgomery and reedman Eric Dolphy, whom Trane had known since the mid-50s, had been added to the quartet. Neither joined the group on a regular basis but, by the following May when Coltrane captured the Arabic feel of flamenco music on the title track of his last Atlantic album *Olé* (using a genuine Spanish folksong waltz, known as *Venga Vallejo* or *El Vito*), Dolphy was contributing to the group full-time. In addition to his flute, bass-clarinet and alto work, he also helped to create the brass-section arrangements when producer Creed Taylor initiated Trane's contract with Impulse Records by recording a big-band album; this contained yet another waltz-time soprano feature intended as a follow-up to *My Favourite Things,* in the shape of the English folksong *Greensleeves*.

But these big-band sessions, which also included a composition by Cal Massey that remained unreleased for many years, were especially notable for Coltrane's own 16-minute piece *Africa*. Although he had previously taken part in recordings with African-related titles by Wilbur Harden and by the Prestige All Stars (arranged by Teddy Charles), he had not as yet created any of his own except for the so-far unissued *Liberia,* which was a thinly disguised version of Dizzy Gillespie's *Night In Tunisia*. Set alongside these relatively conventional performances, the title track of 'Africa/Brass' with its semi-improvised background parts is far more expressionist and 'collectivist' than any previous jazz, except perhaps for some of Mingus's and Sun Ra's pieces. Again, compared with what was being achieved by Ornette Coleman—who was receiving all the critical praise while Coltrane gained the popularity—it still seems remarkably unorthodox and fresh. It is also perhaps Trane's first response on records to the growing unrest among America's black population, but this was not an explicit aspect of its marketing and it was the quality of his music that made Coltrane a reluctant figurehead. Especially the questing, anguished tone of both his tenor and soprano work, full of upper partials and thus reminiscent of the nasal sound of Asian and North African reed instruments, spoke directly not only to blacks but also to those whites who were aware that the Establishment was not exactly on their side.

The full ferocity of Coltrane's solo playing, however, was not completely captured until the Village Vanguard session mentioned above. A career landmark in much the same way as Sonny Rollins's recording at the same club four years earlier, this was Trane's—as it had been Rollins's—first live album of any kind (the ones with the Miles Davis group, even those done officially for Columbia, were not released until much later). The material includes some original compositions similar to the 1960 quartet recordings, although with the addition of Eric Dolphy (i.e. *Spritual* and *India,* the latter dedicated in all likelihood to Cal Massey's daughter rather than the subcontinent of the same name). But the most remarkable performances are *Chasin' The Trane* and *Impressions,* on each of which Coltrane soloes without a break for 15 minutes, driven mercilessly by the up-tempo drumming of Elvin Jones; the continuous cross-rhythms create a dialogue described by some as hysterical, but in hindsight it seems like the sermon of a two-headed angel of vengeance.

Certainly it was not something that European audiences were prepared for, not even those who had heard him with Miles just over eighteen months earlier, when the Coltrane quintet with Eric Dolphy undertook their first overseas tour immediately after the Vanguard recordings. Nor was the seemingly superhuman way in which the soloists, and especially the rhythm-section, could go on expending huge amounts of physical energy for up to half-an-hour without any let-up, although this time-span was mild compared to some of their later American club appearances. Educator Jerry Coker, himself a saxophonist, has written that 'One long, intense solo like Trane's can bring about any or all of the following conditions, sometimes after the end of the solo: (1) heavy breathing, (2) drenching perspiration, (3) trembling, (4) nausea (from tensing stomach muscles to drive air through the horn, not, it is hoped, nausea from nervousness or because of the quality of the solo), (5) uncontrollable exhilaration, (6) fatigue, (7) depression, and (8) muscular tension (residual) and soreness . . . If we could measure the energy level for a given duration, say, for one 32-measure chorus by each artist, and then measure and compare Trane's energy output to that of Lester Young, for example, Trane's level would probably be somewhere between five and ten times greater.'

Coltrane's usual comment was that the effort involved was not conscious when the performance was going well, sometimes expressing the feeling that it was 'God who creates the music and I am only the vehicle'. In an interview following the trip to Europe, he explained that 'Actually, while a guy is soloing, there are many things that happen. Probably he himself doesn't know how many moods or themes he's created. But I think it really ends up with the listener. You know, you hear different people say, "Man, I felt this while he was playing," or "I thought about this." . . . I guess I was on my way

The John Coltrane Quartet in 1962: McCoy Tyner, John Coltrane, Jimmy Garrison and Elvin Jones
Photo: Duncan Schiedt (Frank Driggs Collection)

in '57, when I started to get myself together musically, although at the time I was working academically and technically. It's just recently that I've tried to become even more aware of this other side—the life side of music.' But this was carefully distinguished from any concept such as the Dadaist idea of 'automatic writing', for elsewhere in the same interview was the comment: 'If I feel like I'm just playing notes . . . maybe I don't feel the rhythm or I'm not in the best shape that I should be when this happens. When I become aware of it in the middle of a solo, I'll try to build things to the point where this inspiration is happening again, where things are spontaneous and not contrived. If it reaches that point again, I feel it can continue—it's alive again. But if it doesn't happen, I'll just quit, bow out.'

The fact that Coltrane's control over his instrument was, if anything, greater than ever before was superbly demonstrated by two albums of standard songs produced by Creed Taylor's successor, Bob Thiele, after Dolphy's departure in 1962. These collections (on which Trane played only tenor, incidentally) were clearly aimed at a willing audience that knew of his reputation and, although hooked by the comparatively mild version of *My Favourite Things* that was available on record, or perhaps by *Naima,* had no patience for his more demanding work. In consequence, on the album entitled 'Ballads' he often stayed closer to the melody than on his frequent earlier recordings of comparable material, concentrating on 'singing' the tunes with his inimitable tone. Indeed, on the second album in question, he chose to feature a vocalist, namely Johnny Hartman who had been a colleague in the Gillespie big band, and consciously or not created a session not only unique in his own output but directly comparable to the Parker recording of *Dark Shadows* with singer Earl Coleman. Trane's continued mastery of ballad playing also came through on two items from the successful 1962 quartet session on which McCoy Tyner was replaced by none other than Duke Ellington. The numbers in question were *My Little Brown Book* (which Duke had previously only recorded for distribution to the Armed Forces in 1945, in other words during Trane's period in the service) and *In A Sentimental Mood,* the latter being strongly associated with his stay in the band of Johnny Hodges, even though not originally written for him. Nor was it written for Coltrane, but he managed to create one of its definitive recordings.

Naturally, this activity was somewhat at a tangent to his normal live performances, in which ballads played a minimal role and, instead, continuous catharsis was the rule. Apart from overseas tours, even a group as famous as Coltrane's had few opportunities to play in a concert setting, and it is surprising that there was not more opposition from nightclub owners to his extended performances. McCoy Tyner commented that 'Usually they liked the music to stop at a certain point, so that they could make more on the drinks. I guess those that were really familiar with the group really didn't care whether he played long or not, because they really respected him and they knew the group would do business, you know.' The same point is also illustrated by an anecdote from Ted Curson: 'After he became very famous, there was a club in Philadelphia called Pep's Showbar that called up Coltrane and said, "Mr. Trane, we'd like you to play a couple of weeks in Philly." And Coltrane was very quiet-spoken, he says, "Well, I'm going to play the job in Philly, but I'll tell you right now I'm going to charge you double what I charge everybody else in the world. And the reason why I'm doing this is because, when I was in Philly starving, you never gave me a job." The guy says "Fine!" The place was packed, the guy made a fortune. But I don't think he even understood what the point was, that Trane was trying to show him that he's the same man that he was, except that now he has a reputation.'

Coltrane may also have been aware of the gap between his live music and his recordings, and to a certain extent the recordings deliberately alternated the pattern of releases between the more conservative collections and the relatively exploratory efforts. Certainly a more conscious combination of familiar and original tunes on the European concert tours of 1962 and 1963 made for a considerable improvement in audience communication—though not in England, sadly, for the agency responsible for booking tours of US jazz groups never repeated their initial experience with Coltrane. But the growing success of the group everywhere else might have alerted the kind of culture-conscious listeners who continually require new directions to the possibility of imminent stagnation in Trane's music. If, however, they suspected him of succumbing to this possibility, they could not have been more wrong.

Chapter Six

The undercurrents of change in Coltrane's music were already stirring in 1963. For one thing, the temporary absence for several months of Elvin Jones, due to a drugs bust, obliged Trane to use the services of drummer Roy Haynes among others. Haynes recorded twice with the quartet during this period, and one of the pieces on which he performed represents the first example, apart from the introduction to *Spiritual*, of an original Coltrane composition designed to be played out-of-tempo. Its title, *After The Rain*, is a reminder of his comment shortly after the first European tour that '(Music is) a reflection of the universe. Like having life in miniature. You just take a situation in life or an emotion you know and put it into music. You take a scene you've seen, for instance, and put it to music . . . I haven't made it yet. But I'm beginning to see how to do it.'

Haynes was especially effective in the way he took over the Elvin Jones role at up-tempo, setting up an exciting intellectual discussion with Trane rather than Elvin's overwhelming oratory; but it was always clear that Elvin would return to his post as soon as he was released. However, the stability of the quartet format on record was not invariably matched by live performances, for Coltrane often added musicians for particular performances. Those he invited to sit in included the San Francisco violinist Mike White, saxophonists Archie Shepp and Roscoe Mitchell and (on trumpet) Ornette Coleman. In addition, despite the sparsity of recorded evidence Eric Dolphy, who died tragically in June 1964, continued to make occasional gigs with the group until as late as 31 December 1963.

That was the date of a New York Philharmonic Hall concert at which Coltrane appeared opposite Art Blakey's Jazz Messengers including Wayne Shorter and a Cecil Taylor Unit that contained Albert Ayler. Interestingly, whereas Shorter was (along with Benny Golson) one of the first young tenor-players to be strongly marked by the Coltrane style before working out a personal variation of it, both Ayler and Shepp were representatives of what seemed like a new generation, inspired by Coltrane and by Ornette but striving for a much more basic and much more aggressive revision of current practices.

In particular, his association with Shepp led Trane to introduce him to Impulse Records who put him under contract, and it also made Trane question many assumptions about his own playing and about his role as a musical figurehead. Shepp's outspoken political comments forced Coltrane to realise that misgivings about the growing racial tension of the early 1960s—misgivings he shared with about 20 million other blacks—should find expression in his music. Yet, despite what has been said about *Africa* and *Chasin' The Trane* and their appropriateness to the early 60s, this had been largely unconscious on Coltrane's part. Back in 1958 he had said of his playing, 'If it is interpreted as angry, it is taken wrong. The only one I'm angry at is myself when I don't make what I'm trying to play . . . Music is the means of expression with strong emotional content. Jazz used to be happy and joyous. I'd like to play happy and joyous.' And, even when he openly allowed the emotional content to become more politically relevant, Coltrane was still a man of peace. As Shepp commented, 'He is the product of that same world which created and consequently murdered Bird, and Shadow Wilson, Billie Holiday, Ernie Henry . . . it attests to something: that he was able to overcome that and become the man that he is. There's no vanity about him at all. And, such as it is, he keeps it pretty much to himself.'

Similarly, such anger as he may have felt was also kept pretty much to himself and, on the one occasion he created a piece with a direct contemporary reference, it was superbly self-controlled. *Alabama,* recorded in November 1963 shortly after the bombing of a black church in Birmingham which took the lives of four children, is one of the most sombre pieces in the whole of jazz, a distillation of Trane's ballad playing with all the romantic undertones uprooted. Oddly, it was first issued in what feels like two separate takes, the first beginning out-of-tempo and then gradually replacing the initial despair with a steady tempo of grim determination, but this is abruptly cut off and the second half (sometimes released on its own) remains out-of-tempo and builds to a single, almost understated cry of anguish on the penultimate chord. Coltrane, the man who was more likely to read his Bible in the back room of a nightclub than to make explicit statements about the racial situation, had published a prayerful meditation rather than a call to arms.

With equal restraint, another change had been negotiated in Trane's personal life in the summer of 1963. Whatever private tension and unhappiness he had experienced, he was also bound to take out on himself rather than those around him and, now that his earnings were becoming quite considerable, he simply made arrangements to maintain and support Naima and Syeeda without sharing their home. Very shortly after moving out, he moved in with Alice McLeod who in 1966 finally became his second wife. Like Louis Armstrong's second wife, Alice was a jazz pianist (working at the time with Terry Gibbs) and, like Lil Armstrong, she was to have a considerable musical influence on her husband. Also, like Coltrane's mother whose name she shared, she may be presumed to have held a strong personal sway over him. It was therefore perhaps appropriate that, whereas Naima, during her eight years with John, had suffered two miscarriages, his union with Alice was blessed in summer 1964 by the birth of John Coltrane Jr. followed a year later by Ravi (named after Ravi Shankar) and eighteen months after that by a third son, Oran.

The sum total of these changes was to accentuate the questing nature of Coltrane's personality and of his music. In 1964 he said to Nat Hentoff, 'I'm still primarily looking into certain sounds, certain scales. Not that I'm sure of what I'm looking for, except that it'll be something that hasn't been played before. I don't know what it is. I know I'll have that feeling when I get it. And, in the process of looking, continual looking, the result in any given performance can be long or short. I never know. It's always one thing leading into another. It keeps evolving, and sometimes it's longer than I actually thought it was while I was playing. When things are constantly happening the piece just doesn't feel that long.' The continual looking which may be described as the spiritual aspect of improvisation, from the point of view of the player, was obviously also an ideal metaphor for the spiritual searching of mankind and, in his last years, Coltrane felt the need to make this absolutely explicit. The initial outlet was the suite 'A Love Supreme', in which his thousands of hours of exploration, on the bandstand and in the private pursuit of perfection, were condensed into a classic consummation. Like few other albums recorded up to that time, it is conceived as a whole (although, as with Mingus's 1963 'Black Saint and the Sinner Lady' done for the same producer, the first side is presented as separate tracks instead of being continuous). The cumulative power of the music is more considerable than any single part, and this can be said despite the 'borrowing' of the second theme for another Charles Lloyd 'original' *Dervish Dance*. In so far as the music is descriptive, its subject matter is indeed a love afair but, as in gospel music, it is an affair with the Almighty—the titles of its individual sections being *Acknowledgement*, *Resolution*, *Pursuance* and *Psalm*. The performance presents the definitive quartet at its peak and this, as well as the avowed extra-musical aim, is why it rapidly became Coltrane's best-selling album, eventually reaching over one million purchasers.

The simplicity of means of 'A Love Supreme', however, were in direct contrast to the next release, which might also be interpreted as having some religious significance, being titled *Ascension*. Certainly it is even more slight in terms of thematic material, but this was a continuous 36-minute improvisation by an 11-piece collective including two trumpeters, two altos and three tenors (Coltrane, Shepp and Pharaoh Sanders, who later in 1965 became a full member of Trane's regular group). Recorded in fact some weeks after Ascension Day, the ensemble nevertheless takes off and becomes a maelstrom of undirected energy, especially so when compared to the sharply focussed *Pursuance* which was in the same key of B-flat minor. As well as the religious parallel there is another political parallel, almost too close for comfort, for the summer of 1965 was to be the summer of the Watts Riots, and the apparent violence of the performance may have lost Trane most of the new audience which had just bought 'A Love Supreme'. But it marked his conversion, a seemingly sudden one in terms of his recording career, to the emergent trend of large horn-dominated groups and their revival of simultaneous improvisation. Richard Williams's comment was, 'It certainly wasn't apparent at the time but *Ascension*—beside opening up a lot of possibilities—also opened up a very wide and not very long blind alley. I think it was very necessary at the time, what it did open up was the possibility of a lot of people blowing together without very much structure beyond that inherent in their own feelings for each other. But it was almost as destructive as it was constructive. In its own right, of course, it's a very moving development.'

Albert Ayler went on record at the time as welcoming this new development, saying 'That *Ascension* is beautiful! Consider Coltrane. There's one of the older guys who was playing bebop but who can feel the spirit of what's happening now. He's trying to reach another peace level. This is a beautiful person, a highly spiritual brother. Imagine being able in one lifetime to move from the kind of peace he found in bebop to a new peace.' But Coltrane's search for new sounds continued abated and, while there is no direct similarity to Ayler in his tenor tone, it had lost its last remnants of astringency and openly incorporated the honking and wailing of his rhythm-and-blues past. Virtually none of his new material involved the soprano any more (although he did eventually make brief use of the bass-clarinet and flute given to him by the late Eric Dolphy's parents), and the addition of new musicians which had once been reserved for live sets now invaded his studio work in albums like 'Om' and 'Kulu Se Mama'. Ted Curson, who apparently refused Trane's invitation to take part in such sessions, told me that 'Without knowing him, you could come in with your horn and say "Can I play?" And he'd say "OK, come on." That's the kind of man he was, he had no fear of anyone. He said "I can always hear something in somebody else that I can use." It's funny, because I couldn't hear anyone who could play anything he could use.'

Up to this point, however, the lynch-pin of all the group's performances was still the ever-expanding musical partnership between Trane and Elvin Jones, as items such as *Pursuance, Amen, Ascension* and the 'Live in Paris' album demonstrate. Elvin himself said 'I knew it was going to be good, that much was obvious. But I didn't really know to what extent, I don't think anyone could probably tell to what length it would actually go.' 'Kulu Se Mama', however, was the session which marked the introduction of a second drummer (Frank Butler) and additional instrumentation such as congas and the *mbira* or thumb-piano. And it was then that the historic rhythm-section began to break up. According to McCoy Tyner, 'Frank Butler and Elvin had played very well together with the two-drummer concept. But then, when Elvin and Rashied Ali played together, it wasn't compatible and I was in the middle of that. If you have two

Alice Coltrane

drummers, they have to work very well together, otherwise it can be overwhelming.' Within a month of Rashied Ali being added to the regular group, Tyner left in December 1965 and was replaced, in what was from some points of view the obvious solution, by Coltrane's musical counsellor and wife-to-be Alice. This change in the piano chair can only have accelerated Elvin's realisation that, if Trane was serious about keeping his new drummer, then Elvin too would have to leave. Which he duly did at the start of March 1966, saying sardonically about Coltrane's latest music, 'Only poets can understand it.'

If it now seemed that the music immediately became more spaced-out, this was nevertheless a process that had already begun during the previous year. And factors such as the vocals of poet Juno Lewis on 'Kulu Se Mama' or the chanting which begins the album 'Om' were hardly encouraging signs. Apparent support for the view that Coltrane lost his musical sense of direction at this point comes from the writer Amiri Baraka (LeRoi Jones), who told Valerie Wilmer that 'The Black Liberation Movement was attacked in the 60s and 70s and our leadership destroyed. But in that stopping of that movement you'll notice also that the music goes through some severe changes. On the one hand it gets to be ultra-metaphysical where you get a lot of "Om-m-m-m-m" in it. And then there's the development of a whole lot of non-blues-oriented "avant-garde".' Both of these trends, especially the former, might be said to have been foreshadowed by Coltrane, in much the same way that *Ascension* predicted the Watts Riots. And, as Richard Williams said, 'There's a case to be made for the supposition that he was the one who really began, or laid the groundwork for, the concept of mammoth rhythm-sections such as Miles Davis uses or like most of the "jazz-funk-fusion-blah-blah" groups.'

If questioned on this point, Coltrane might well have said that he was merely seeking to reconcile opposing tendencies, but perhaps this was precisely because he could not foresee the direction of his own music, or that of black music in general. Nat Hentoff has described how, at this period, he 'would practice for hours, sometimes silently—just running his fingers over the keys—and pick up new instruments and meditate and listen to recordings of Indian music and the music of South African Pygmies'. Certainly there was no lessening of Coltrane's demands on his stamina when playing in public, and if anything the driven quality of his improvisations seemed even more marked. Jerry Coker, confirming like all of his fellow reedmen the superb instrumental control that Coltrane demonstrated even in his wildest moments, recalled the parable of the film *The Red Shoes*: 'A young woman . . . puts on the shoes (and) is compelled to dance vigorously and joyously; and when she tires, the red shoes will not permit her to stop dancing, not even long enough to take off the shoes, and so she dances to exhaustion and death.'

Exactly when Coltrane became aware that he was seriously ill is not known. But Johnny Griffin, discussing the extreme nature of his latter-day style, related it not only to social forces but to Trane's personal condition. 'Coltrane, to me, was one of the great musicians in jazz of all times. A beautiful person to know, to be around, and the man really had everything to work with. I mean, what he saw or what he envisioned with his music towards the middle 60s before his death, who knows? Maybe that has something pertaining to the future of the way people are feeling. But the music to me was like pathos, it was like he was being tortured. In fact, I had the feeling that he knew of his eventual demise, and it was painful for him to accept it.' If this was true in any literal way, Coltrane certainly gave no hint to his closest associates. McCoy Tyner knew only that 'For a while, he was on health foods. He was that kind of a person, once he got involved in something, he would come off the diet and then he'd go back. He would gain weight, then lose weight again.' It was only much later that Rashied Ali, who had used the occasion of the group's Japanese tour in July 1966 to take frequent snapshots, became aware that all those featuring Coltrane show him holding a hand against the area of his liver. But it is true that, when he accepted a European tour for November 1966, he felt unable to honour the invitation and was replaced by the groups of Sonny Rollins and Albert Ayler. Even within the United States, he undertook fewer and fewer engagements, and many which had been agreed for the first half of 1967 were in the event cancelled.

John Coltrane died of cancer of the liver on 17 July 1967. A year earlier in Japan, he had been asked what he would like to be in ten years' time and had replied 'I would like to be a saint'. For all practical purposes, it took far less than ten years to achieve this goal. Alice Coltrane undoubtedly helped in the process of canonisation, partly through becoming a bandleader in her own right and partly through authorising the regular issue of previously unreleased Impulse recordings. Fortunately, she never repeated the gross artistic miscalculation whereby the 1965-66 album 'Infinity' was issued in 1972 with the overdubbing of strings, her own harp and vibes playing, a second bass (Charlie Haden), and Indian tambura, and bells played by the five-year-old Oran Coltrane; of this travesty, Rashied Ali said 'It's like rewriting the Bible'. Perhaps, in fact, it was more akin to the Apocrypha, the existence of which has done nothing to discredit the more universally accepted biblical writings, just as those responsible for issuing unauthorised recordings may recall the money-changers in the temple who inadvertently highlighted the incorruptibility of another man with the initials J.C. The power of the music left by Coltrane, whether preserved in its original forms or filtered through its incredible wide influence on other performers, will inspire due reverence and awe for a very long time to come.

Chapter Seven

As previously mentioned, Coltrane's influence on other musicians has been extremely widespread, and as a result is largely concerned with generalities. These include such fundamentals as the philosophical underpinning of his musical approach and the related question of what might be jocularly called 'attitude to the job'. In these respects Coltrane set a supremely demanding example to his disciples, most of whom have come nowhere near to meeting his standards.

The actual detail of his playing, however, has proved so inescapable in itself that it provides the best basis for recognising his influence on others, and for understanding exactly how that influence touched more and more performers as Coltrane's style developed. This immediately raises the problem that it is impossible to speak in terms of a single style, as is demonstrated by the fact that each new manifestation of his individual development between 1956 and 1966 has had, and continues to have, its own followers. To this extent, it will be necessary to use the shorthand technique of describing different stylistic 'phases', while bearing in mind constantly that this is a distortion of the reality. For, even if the various followers insist that such-and-such a phase was an unwelcome or even unnatural development in terms of Coltrane's music, nevertheless the stylistic changes formed a seamless (or at least continuous) progression; and, furthermore, the chronology and the stylistic discrepancies of records have done much to create the false impression of a 'versatile' chameleon, taking on the protective colouring of different jazz genres.

Nevertheless Coltrane, more than most jazz players, saw music as being indivisible and was perfectly able to involve himself successively in the convoluted catharsis of *Chasin' The Trane* and the reflective romanticism of the 'Ballads' album.

It is easy enough, in retrospect, to see that Coltrane was advancing on all fronts and that his painstakingly assembled innovations were all part of one long process. At the time of his first maturity, however, one observer summarised how far he had come already. Writing in late 1958, no less a person than pianist Cecil Taylor devoted 600 words to reviewing Trane's newest recording, and included the following comments: 'Coltrane at times seems to play away from everyone rhythmically, and yet his line has a time that is angular and evil and laden with its own rhythm. His playing sometimes becomes a mirror of the past reminding one of the precision of Benny Carter, Stitt and Gordon of the late 40s, with the texture of Pres (Lester Young). His interval conception is a whole one as he utilises large and small intervals. He uses the entire range of his horn. In ballads, he ventures into areas of sound that are uncommon. One is reminded of Hodges, his security of tone in the higher registers. Also, the vocal feeling of Eckstine and Sarah (Vaughan). In his blues playing there is Bird as well as Rollins. In short his expression is a beautiful and meaningful one.'

Of the various factors mentioned by Taylor in this extract, it was the 'uncommon areas of sound' which initially provoked the strongest reactions. And, because Coltrane's tone has become so widespread and acceptable since at least the 1960s, it requires an effort of historical imagination to realise what hostility it aroused. Sy Johnson's comment about 'trouble with his reed' is not irrelevant here for, especially in the early recordings with Miles Davis which were most people's introduction to Trane, the two factors can not always be easily separated from each other. But, such occasional difficulties aside, it is obvious that his tone was absolutely unique and, indeed, even the rare early live albums with Gillespie and Hodges show him already aiming clearly in this direction. As Nat Hentoff has written more recently, 'Lester Young was in disfavour among some of his peers for quite a while because his sound was too "light" compared to Coleman Hawkins's robust fullness . . . At the advent of Charlie Parker one of the many criticisms of his playing by older musicians and by traditionalist listeners was that his tone was "bad", too acrid by contrast, say, with that of Johnny Hodges. In the case of John Coltrane, a majority of the initial reviews of his recordings . . . also cited his "strident", "unpleasant" sound. Mine were among them.'

The Trane 'sound' that is most usually associated with him is probably that of 1958-59, when his fluency and articulation (and reeds) had become totally infallible, and the tone completely consistent and consequently more identifiable. It has, on the one hand, a warmth and power which is quite easily masked, on the other hand, by that hard thin edge, already suggesting the soprano saxophone before he actually took up the instrument; and it has the odd sensation of a gap in the centre between the one hand and the other, which is perhaps explained by the actual configuration of upper partials in the sound. But it should not be forgotten that the sound continued to evolve and change—indeed, after taking up the soprano, he once said 'You need to play it with such a tight embouchure that I've been frightened of losing my tenor embouchure'. By 1961, however, when that statement was made, the tenor sound was gradually becoming more vocalised, enhanced by hints of vibrato and special tonal effects created by 'false fingerings', a technique first exploited by Lester Young. Interestingly, Trane's soprano tone never developed much, and in fact its use gradually decreased whereas by 1965 the previous tendencies of the tenor tone had become much more marked. And the deliberately hoarse quality of the lowest and the highest notes only mirrors a general metamorphosis over the whole range into an extraordinary plangent wail, which has not been reproduced by anyone else.

Rhythmically, Coltrane's development was perhaps even more varied and, in its early stages, might have seemed to justify charges of incompetence. This was doubtless because of his attempts to use the rhythmic legacy of Lester Young and Lester-influenced Dexter Gordon as a vehicle for the much greater urgency conveyed by Parker. However, by the time he had mastered the necessary fluency to emulate Parker if he so wished, he was aiming for a different kind of urgency. Not only was the phraseology sometimes even more densely packed with notes but, as a result, the rhythmic outline was less obvious and less varied than Parker's had been; the note groupings described as 'sheets of sound' may have been irregular, but the lack of strong accentuation made them seem a regular and unstoppable flow. It was only in the 1960s that more rhythmic definition was introduced by breaking up the flow in a way that felt appropriate and natural, thanks to the collaboration of Elvin Jones, rather than 'away from everyone' in the group (as previously described by Cecil Taylor). At least at up-tempo, this process tended towards extreme fragmentation near the end of Coltrane's career, in a way which only made sense because of the cumulative effect of the very lengthy solos he espoused, and which strongly contrasted with the subtle rhythmic waves engendered in his slow or out-of-tempo improvisation.

Of course, these rhythmic factors were closely allied both to the melodic lines he chose to employ at various stages, and the relationship of the lines to the types of material he created. As previously noted, there is not much sign of originality in Trane's solo work (his tone apart) during his earliest recordings. But, by the time his original approach really came together in the late 1950s, the scale-derived and broken-chord passages were only distantly connected with the styles of his first models, and were a translation of aspects of his practice methods into a genuine form of expression. Similar things had earlier been said of Parker and Gillespie but, in Coltrane's case, there was a period dominated by series of bars filled with eighth-notes and with regular, almost European-style, accents on the first and third beats. (It is worth noting that this particular Coltrane approach is the one which is most suitable to improvising in the 'jazz-funk-fusion-blah-blah' idiom, and which may indeed have provoked the expansion of the rhythm-section in that idiom.) Miles Davis, speaking of Trane in 1958, said 'He's been working on those arpeggios and playing them fifty different ways and playing them all at once. However, he *is* beginning to leave more space—except when he gets nervous. . .. What he does is to play five notes of a chord and then keep changing it around, trying to see how many different ways it can sound. It's like explaining something five different ways.'

According to the evidence of contemporary recordings and of eyewitness accounts, this approach crystallised during Coltrane's brief tenure with Thelonious Monk. And, of course, it is singularly appropriate to the performance of Trane's first important batch of original compositions, conceived around the same time and typified by *Giant Steps*. The germ of this tune's harmonic cycle, although it can be heard in the 1937 Rodgers and Hart song *Have You Met Miss Jones?*, was most probably first suggested to Coltrane by the flattened-fifth substitutions in Monk's *Bemsha Swing* and in the Tadd Dameron and Miles Davis companion pieces, *Lady Bird* and *Half Nelson*—indeed, Trane's own *Lazy*(sic) *Bird* begins with an early development of the same germ. As well as *Giant Steps* itself, Coltrane made use of the same cycle in, among others, *Countdown* (based on *Tune Up*), *Satellite* (ditto *How High The Moon*), *Exotica/Untitled Original* (ditto *I Can't Get Started*, *26–2*, *But Not For Me*, and briefly in *Body And Soul* and *The Night Has A Thousand Eyes*. But in all of these apart from the last two, and especially in *Giant Steps*, this new method of changing keys taxed the composer's ingenuity in circumventing its restrictions to such an extent that one musician described him as sounding 'like a rat in a maze'.

This highly evolved harmonic scheme also seems to be at exactly the opposite extreme from the idea of a 'pedal point', i.e. a continuously repeated bass note implying the total lack of harmonic movement for several bars at a stretch. Already heard in the Miles Davis version of *Dear Old Stockholm* and in certain Mingus pieces, this was employed by Coltrane as early as the recordings of *Nita* (1956) and *Moment's Notice* (1957) and in his arrangements of standards such as *While My Lady Sleeps*. It was this development which led to the completely scale-orientated (i.e. 'modal') compositions such as Davis's *Milestones* and *So What*. Coltrane initially adopted this approach to throw new light on the time-honoured 12-bar blues, as in *Equinox, Mr. Day, Mr. Knight* and *Village Blues* (which has a similar bass-figure to *While My Lady*). Yet another variation of the same bass-figure, however, inaugurated the beneficial compromise between these two apparently conflicting approaches, in the fascinating *Fifth House*. Despite being derived from the A/A/B/A standard *What Is This Thing Called Love?* the harmonic movement of the A sections is replaced by the bass pedal-point, whereas the B section's rate of harmonic change is actually increased by the incorporation of a *Giant Steps* cycle. Coltrane's A section improvisations, however, use the static bass part as a foundation for the superimposition of a continuous series of implied key-changes. This technique, which came to be known as 'side-slipping', eventually became his preferred method of balancing the beneficial open-ended quality of modal materials with the avoidance of boredom, by reference to basic principles of harmonic tension and release. Composer George Russell virtually predicted as much when saying in 1960, 'This is what Coltrane in his playing is illuminating, the vertical, the chromatic relationship to the chord. X number of chords upon one single chord . . . Trane knows the chord exists but he also seems to sense that there is a whole unexplored universe that that chord implies.'

Let us now step back and compare this approach in Coltrane's later work with earlier performances. *Pursuance* (from 'A Love Supreme') has already been mentioned as a prime example of the partnership between Trane and Elvin Jones, and it is also one of the last examples of the saxophonist playing a 12-bar blues. Its hectic tempo of nearly 300 bars to the minute during the main tenor solo places it in the same category as the almost as fast *Locomotion* (on the 1957 album 'Blue Train'). Actually *Locomotion,* like the much slower *Traneing In* of a month earlier, has a 44-bar chorus derived from Lester Young's *D.B. Blues* and thus includes a non-blues middle-eight, but the 12-bar sections comprising the majority of the piece are entirely typical of Coltrane's blues playing at this period. Although, rhythmically, there are already hints of the continuous eighth-notes accented on beats one and three, much of the general vocabulary is straight out of Parker and Dexter Gordon, prime examples being the 'turnarounds' at the end of each of Coltrane's solo choruses. Undoubtedly this is encouraged by the traditional nature of the blues form, and indeed the opening bars after the ensemble chorus can be heard as a quotation from *After Hours;* this and a later blues quotation deliberately contrast with the bebop or hard-bop feeling of the rest. By comparison, *Pursuance* employs even simpler means but with far greater intensity. Jerry Coker's description of the Coltrane improvisation after the piano solo points out that the first 50-plus bars from the tenor are all based exclusively on the same five-note scale. The variations of pitch and tone, later augmented by alternate fingerings, lead to momentary changes of key (i.e. side-slipping) which grow progressively more frequent as the solo continues. And the gradual increase in rhythmic fragmentation builds the momentum to such a stage that the conventional repeat of the theme at the end is clearly insufficient to resolve the tension.

Surprisingly, the harmonic aspect is also less to the fore in Coltrane's treatment of the genre usually thought of as most harmonically-orientated, the slow ballad. The 1958 version of Billy Eckstine's *I Want To Talk About You* (part of the album which Cecil Taylor was reviewing) may be taken as typical of the early Coltrane

John Coltrane Photo: Val Wilmer

ballad style. While not devoid of interesting harmonic twists, again usually during turnarounds at the ends of sections, the approach is above all surprisingly melodic. Even the second, more improvisational chorus contains frequent long notes, which Trane 'sings' in his uniquely personal tone, joined by brief linking passages. What is more surprising, though, is the retention of this approach in later ballads, for instance the 1963 'Live At Birdland' version of the same tune. The level of complexity is certainly greater from the outset and, as the performance progresses, there is similar rhythmic fragmentation to that of *Pursuance;* but the harmonic emphasis is slight indeed, until the closing 2½ minutes of completely solo tenor where Coltrane seems to accompany his own melodic improvisation with broken chords and bass notes, for all the world like Art Tatum or some other piano soloist. Comparison between the two versions is rendered more striking by the earlier record's anti-climatic piano and bass choruses, whereas the 1963 performance features Coltrane throughout, first responding to the ever-increasing activity of the rhythm-section and then to their silence, as he elaborates the last 16 bars of a chorus out-of-tempo without decreasing the intensity.

Finally, when it comes to Coltrane's individual angle on the non-harmonic material of modal tunes, it is instructive to be able to go back to the 1956 *Dear Old Stockholm* with Davis. As well as the various pedal-point sections added by Miles, the original Swedish folksong itself strongly suggests the use of the Aeolian Mode, irrespective of the simple chord-changes which accompany it. Although Trane's style was still somewhat unformed, this track contains one of his best early solos, yet it finds him ignoring the modal implications eagerly seized on by Miles. Instead, he uses his knowledge of scales and arpeggios to improvise directly on the harmonic cadences of the chord-sequence, sounding alternately frustrated and inspired by the brevity of the pedal points, one of which is the occasion for a quotation from *While My Lady Sleeps* (bars 21–24). The 1959 *So What,* on the other hand, seems much more suited to his developing approach. In the same key as *Dear Old Stockholm,* it is a 32-bar A/A/B/A tune entirely in the Dorian Mode, with only one change to the same mode a semitone higher for the B section, and it inspires Coltrane to a full exploration of his resources at this stage. He sticks very closely to the notes permitted by the mode, introducing only occasional passing-notes, and manages to achieve considerable variety in his melodic and rhythmic shapes which build to a climax shortly before the end of the solo, in a manner undoubtedly learned directly from Miles.

Impressions, again in the same key, is Coltrane's own reworking of *So What,* with a theme from Morton Gould's *Pavanne* as the melody for the A section (an idea credited to Pete LaRoca, incidentally, when it was first recorded some nine months before Coltrane, under the title *Why Not?*) and with the B section melody taken from the *Pavane* by Ravel, sometimes known as *The Lamp Is Low*(!) Trane's first recording, on the album of the same name, is a tour-de-force of continuous improvisation during which the saxophonist completes 31 choruses of solo work between the opening and closing themes. The way in which the improvisation is developed provides an excellent example of the special conditions governing this sort of extended exploration. The first chorus after the theme includes some passing notes, although basically concentrating on the Dorian scale, and already there are uses of alternate fingering to give different densities to adjacent notes (some equivalent phrases from a Stockholm concert recording of three weeks later, listed as (44) in the discography, are transcribed in David Baker's monograph on Coltrane). The second chorus, played with a broader and more even tone, has much deliberately repetitive phrasing accenting the 1st and 3rd beats, while the following chorus caps this with frequent side-slipping into other keys. Interestingly, the fourth chorus (after which McCoy Tyner drops out of the accompaniment) reverts to the repetitive accenting and the fifth again turns to side-slipping, before the sixth and seventh choruses combine all the previously mentioned features with gradually longer and more relaxed phrases. A kind of plateau is reached where the eighth chorus introduces much simpler, more overtly melodic material in order to relaunch the various permutations which then recur and take the solo to new heights, followed by new plateaus and yet more heights. While specific details of later moments would be worth drawing attention to, it is the overall impact of the solo which is more striking than any of the details.

If this original *Impressions* is a strong emotional experience for most listeners even today, then a later version such as the 1965 'Live In Paris' recording is something else again. Coltrane takes a much shorter solo of only 12½ choruses but the mood is immediately darker and more anguished. Supported by seemingly never-ending and never-resolving discords from Tyner, and drumming from Jones which resembles a soundtrack for the Vietnam War, Trane becomes involved in deliberate tonal distortions as early as the end of the first chorus. And, although one or two similarities of construction to the 1961 version can be discerned, the whole intent of the performance is seemingly to obscure the structure with uncontainable emotion. Yet, while the tenor sound sometimes resembles aspects of both Archie Shepp and Albert Ayler, it is clear that this is still Coltrane and no one else.

Whether or not this period of his work is what he will be remembered for, no one else had developed continuously from a bebop-derived style to the outer reaches of free-jazz in this logical but dramatic way. It is a drama which brings us back to the nature of his search and its relevance to the times in which he lived. But, even more so, it reminds us that he transcended those times. As Don Cherry put it, 'When he came on the scene, he realised that he had to carry the message, and he carried it very well. His thinking was spiritual but instead of speaking it, he would play and you could feel it.'

Discography

In the chronological listing which follows, I have shown virtually everything issued so far featuring John Coltrane. Also included are the details of known unissued material from studio sessions, but for reasons of space I have omitted unissued 'live' recordings and even unissued tracks from concerts which have been partly issued.

All items obtainable currently or on recently available releases are also cross-referenced to the separate list of albums at the end of the discography. As with all discographies, however, there is a strong possibility that this aspect of the work will rapidly be outdated by the deletion of some albums, their re-issue with new catalogue numbers, or the releasing of material presently unavailable. It is hoped that at least the following pages provide an adequate guide to Coltrane's huge output and, as is only natural, I am grateful for the assistance of previous discographies, and also especially to Bruce Bastin, Tony Middleton, Bob Porter, Tony Russell and Chris Sheridan.

The abbreviations used are as follows:- (arr) arranger, (as) alto saxophone, (b) bass, (bars) baritone saxophone, (bcl) bass-clarinet, (btb) bass-trombone, (cbsn) contrabassoon, (cel) cello, (cl) clarinet, (cnt) cornet, (cond) conductor, (D) Dutch, (d) drums, (E) English, (euph) euphonium, (F) French, (f) flute, (flh) fluegelhorn, (fr-h) french-horn, (G) German, (g) guitar, (I) Italian, (narr) narrator, (org) organ, (p) piano, (perc) percussion, (picc) piccolo, (ss) soprano saxophone, (tb) trombone, (t) trumpet, (ts) tenor saxophone, (tu) tuba, (vcl) vocal, (vib) vibraphone, (vla) viola, (vln) violin, *incomplete recording.

BRIAN PRIESTLEY, London, August 1986

DIZZY GILLESPIE AND HIS ORCHESTRA

Dizzy Gillespie (t, vcl), Elmon Wright, Willie Cook, Don Slaughter (t), Matthew Gee, Sam Hurt, Charles Greenlee (Harnifan Majid) (tb), Jimmy Heath, John Coltrane (as), Jesse Powell, Paul Gonsalves (ts), Al Gibson (bars), John Acea (p), John Collins/Floyd Smith (g), Al McKibbon (b), Specs Wright (d), Carlos Duchesne, Francisco Pozo (perc), Tiny Irvin, Joe Carroll (vcl)

NYC, November 21, 1949/January 9, 1950

8 tracks recorded for Capitol

DIZZY GILLESPIE SEXTET

Dizzy Gillespie (t), John Coltrane (ts), Milt Jackson (vib), Billy Taylor (p), Percy Heath (b), Art Blakey (d) *Birdland, NYC, January 6, 1951*

	CONGO BLUES/YESTERDAYS	Oberon 5100
	NIGHT IN TUNISIA	(1) "

Birdland, NYC, January 13, 1951

	BIRKS' WORKS	(2) Duke D1019
	GOOD BAIT	(1, 2) Oberon 5100

Birdland, NYC, January 20, 1951

	I CAN'T GET STARTED/JUMPIN' WITH SYMPHONY SID	Oberon 5100

Jimmy Foreman (p) replaces Taylor *Birdland, NYC, February 3, 1951*

	BIRKS' WORKS	Oberon 5100

As for January 6 except Kenny Burrell (g), Kansas Fields (d) replace Taylor and Blakey, Freddy Strong (vcl-1) *Detroit, March 1, 1951*

4000	LOVE ME PRETTY BABY -1,2	unissued (?)
4010	WE LOVE TO BOOGIE -1,3	(3) Dee Gee 3600
4015	TIN TIN DEO -4	(3) Dee Gee 3601
4020	BIRKS' WORKS	(3) "

2-Gillespie out, 3-Jackson plays p, 4-The Calypso Boys (perc) added

As for March 1 except John Lewis (p) replaces Burrell, J.J. Johnson (tb) added

Birdland, NYC, March 17, 1951

	BIRKS' WORKS	(1) Oberon 5100

GAY CROSSE AND HIS GOOD HUMOR SIX

James Robertson (t), John Coltrane (as, ts), Gay Crosse (ts, vcl-1), Charles Ross (p), John Lathan (b), Specs Wright (d) *Philadelphia, January 19, 1952*

GC1	FAT SAM FROM BIRMINGHAM-1	Gotham 276
GC2	BITTERSWEET	"
	SLOW AND EAST/NO BETTER FOR YOU	unissued

Note: Coltrane may be included in the Gay Crosse personnel which backed Christine Kittrell on GOTTA STOP LOVING YOU (Republic 7062) (3a). Members of this group may also have recorded uncredited behind Charles Ruckles on I GOT A FEELIN' (Speed 300) (3b), where Coltrane appears to be responsible for two phrases in the closing vocal chorus.

EARL BOSTIC AND HIS ORCHESTRA
Gene Redd (t, vib), Blue Mitchell (t), Earl Bostic, Pinky Williams (as), John Coltrane (ts), Joe Knight (p), Jimmy Shirley/Harold Grant (g), Ike Isaacs (b), Specs Wright (d), unknown vcl-group on one track (probably including Coltrane)
Cincinnatti, April 7/August 15, 1952
8 tracks recorded for King

JOHNNY HODGES AND HIS ORCHESTRA
Prob. Emmett Berry (t), Lawrence Brown (tb), Johnny Hodges (as), John Coltrane (ts), prob. Richie Powell (p), John Williams (b), prob. Jimmy Johnson (d), unknown vcl -1
Unknown location, poss. January 1954

	THROUGH FOR THE NIGHT (SIDEWAYS)	(1) Enigma 1052
	CASTLE ROCK	”
	IN A MELLOTONE	(1) Swing Treasury 109
	I'VE GOT A MIND TO RAMBLE BLUES -1	Enigma 1052
	DON'T CRY BABY BLUES -1	”
	BURGUNDY WALK (RAB 'N TRANE) (GLOBETROTTER)	Swing Treasury 109
	DON'T BLAME ME	(1) Enigma 1052

Harold Baker (t), Call Cobbs (p), Louie Bellson (d) replace Berry, Powell and Johnson
NYC, July 2, 1954

1860	BURGUNDY WALK	(4) Norgran 122
1861	ON THE SUNNY SIDE OF THE STREET	(4) Norgran 131

Note: Coltrane replaced by Jimmy Hamilton (ts, cl) and Harry Carney (bars) on other titles from this session; date has also been given as August 5

MILES DAVIS QUINTET
Miles Davis (t), John Coltrane (ts), Red Garland (p), Paul Chambers (b), Philly Joe Jones (d)
NYC, October 27, 1955

CO54129	TWO BASS HIT	(5) Columbia KC2 36278
CO54130	AH-LEU-CHA	(6) Columbia CL949
CO54131	BILLY BOY -1	unissued
CO54132	LITTLE MELONAE	(7) Columbia KC32025
CO54133	BUDO (i.e. HALLUCINATIONS)	(7) Columbia CL1020

Hackensack, N.J., November 16, 1955

814	STABLEMATES	(8) Prestige PRLP7014
815	HOW AM I TO KNOW?	(8) ”
816	JUST SQUEEZE ME	(8) ”
818	MILES' THEME (THE THEME)	(8) ”
819	S'POSIN'	(8) ”

1-prob. Garland, Chambers and Jones only
Note: Coltrane out on 817

PAUL CHAMBERS SEXTET

Curtis Fuller (tb), John Coltrane (ts), Pepper Adams (bars), Roland Alexander (p-1), Paul Chambers (b), Philly Joe Jones (d) *poss. Detroit, November 1955*

	TRANE'S STRAIN	Transition LP30
	HIGH STEP	Blue Note BN-LA451-H2
	NIXON, DIXON AND YATES BLUES-1	"

Note: There is strong circumstantial evidence that this session was held in Boston, and though the alternative date of April 20, 1955 is implausible, April 20, *1956* has also been suggested

PAUL CHAMBERS QUARTET

John Coltrane (ts) Kenny Drew (p), Paul Chambers (b), Philly Joe Jones (d) *Los Angeles, March 1956*

DEXTERITY/STABLEMATES/EASY TO LOVE/JOHN PAUL JONES/EASTBOUND Jazz-West LP7

Note: Coltrane out on remaining track

ELMO HOPE SEXTET—INFORMAL JAZZ

Donald Byrd (t), Hank Mobley, John Coltrane (ts), Elmo Hope (p), Paul Chambers (b), Philly Joe Jones (d) *Hackensack, N.J., May 7, 1956*

884	WEE JAH	(9) Prestige PRLP7043
885	POLKA DOTS AND MOONBEAMS	(9) "
886	ON IT	(9) "
887	AVALON	(9) "

MILES DAVIS QUINTET

As November 16, 1955 *Hackensack, N.J., May 11, 1956*

888	IN YOUR OWN SWEET WAY	(10) Prestige PRLP7166
889	DIANE	(10) Prestige PRLP7200
890	TRANE'S BLUES (i.e. JOHN PAUL JONES)	(10) Prestige PRLP7166
892	IT COULD HAPPEN TO YOU	(10a) Prestige PRLP7129
893	WOODY'N YOU	(10a) "
895	THE SURREY WITH THE FRINGE ON TOP	(10) Prestige PRLP7200
896	IT NEVER ENTERED MY MIND	(10) Prestige 45-165, PRLP7166
898	SALT PEANUTS	(10) Prestige PRLP7200
899	FOUR	(10) Prestige PRLP7166
900	THE THEME I	(10) "
901	THE THEME II	(10) "

Note: Coltrane out on 891, 894, 896 (except for last chord) and 897

SONNY ROLLINS—TENOR MADNESS

As last session except Sonny Rollins (ts) replaces Davis

Hackensack, N.J., May 24, 1956

906	TENOR MADNESS	(10b) Prestige PRLP7047

MILES DAVIS QUINTET—ROUND ABOUT MIDNIGHT

As before *NYC, June 5, 1956*

CO56090	DEAR OLD STOCKHOLM	(6) Columbia CL949
CO56091	BYE BYE BLACKBIRD	(6) ”
CO56092	TADD'S DELIGHT (i.e. SID'S DELIGHT)	(6) ”

PRESTIGE ALL STARS—TENOR CONCLAVE

Al Cohn, John Coltrane, Hank Mobley, Zoot Sims (ts), Red Garland (p), Paul Chambers (b), Art Taylor (d) *Hackensack, N.J., September 7, 1956*

975	JUST YOU, JUST ME	(11) Prestige PRLP7074
976	TENOR CONCLAVE	(11) ”
977	HOW DEEP IS THE OCEAN	(11) ”
978	BOB'S BOYS	(11) ”

MILES DAVIS QUINTET—ROUND ABOUT MIDNIGHT

As before *NYC, September 10, 1956*

CO56584	ALL OF YOU	(6) Columbia B9491, CL949
CO56585	SWEET SUE	(7) Columbia CL919
CO56586	'ROUND MIDNIGHT	(6) Columbia B9491, CL949

PAUL CHAMBERS SEXTET—WHIMS OF CHAMBERS

Donald Byrd (t), John Coltrane (ts), Horace Silver (p), Kenny Burrell (g), Paul Chambers (b), Philly Joe Jones (d) *Hackensack, N.J., September 21, 1956*

OMICRON/NITA/WE SIX/JUST FOR LOVE/DEAR ANN Blue Note BLP1534

Note: Coltrane out on two further tracks.

MILES DAVIS QUINTET

As before *Hackensack, N.J., October 26, 1956*

995	IF I WERE A BELL	(10a) Prestige 45-123, PRLP7129
996	WELL YOU NEEDN'T	(10) Prestige PRLP7200
997	'ROUND MIDNIGHT	(11a) Prestige PRLP7150
998	HALF NELSON	(10) Prestige PRLP7166
999	YOU'RE MY EVERYTHING	(10a) Prestige PRLP7129
1000	I COULD WRITE A BOOK	(10a) ”
1001	OLEO	(10a) ”
1002	AIREGIN	(10a) Prestige PRLP7094
1003	TUNE UP	(10a) ”
1004	WHEN LIGHTS ARE LOW	(10a) ”
1005	BLUES BY FIVE	(10a) ”

Note: Coltrane out on 1006 (MY FUNNY VALENTINE)

TADD DAMERON QUARTET

John Coltrane (ts), Tadd Dameron (p), John Simmons (b), Philly Joe Jones (d)

Hackensack, N.J., November 30, 1956

1025	MATING CALL	(11)	Prestige PRLP7070
1026	SOULTRANE	(11)	”
1027	GNID	(11)	”
1028	SUPER JET	(11)	”
1029	ON A MISTY NIGHT	(11)	”
1030	ROMAS	(11)	”

MILES DAVIS QUINTET

As before *Blue Note, Philadelphia, December 8, 1956*

TUNE UP/WALKIN' (ROYAL GARDEN BLUES) (1) Teppa 76

PRESTIGE ALL STARS—INTERPLAY FOR TWO TRUMPETS AND TWO SAXOPHONES

Idrees Sulieman (t), Webster Young (cnt), John Coltrane, Bobby Jaspar (ts), Mal Waldron (p, arr), Kenny Burrell (g), Paul Chambers (b), Art Taylor (d)

Hackensack, N.J., March 22, 1957

1163	ANATOMY	(12)	Prestige PRLP7112
1164	INTERPLAY	(12)	”
1165	LIGHT BLUE	(12)	”
1166	SOUL EYES	(12)	”
1167	C.T.A. -1	(12)	Prestige PRLP7117

1-Coltrane, Red Garland (p), Chambers and Taylor only on this track

JOHNNY GRIFFIN—A BLOWIN' SESSION

Lee Morgan (t), Johnny Griffin, Hank Mobley, John Coltrane (ts), Wynton Kelly (p), Paul Chambers (b), Art Blakey (d) *Hackensack, N.J., April 6, 1957*

THE WAY YOU LOOK TONIGHT/BALL BEARING/ALL THE THINGS YOU ARE/ SMOKE STACK Blue Note BLP1559

THELONIOUS MONK—THELONIOUS HIMSELF

John Coltrane (ts), Thelonious Monk (p), Wilbur Ware (b) *NYC, April 16, 1957*

MONK'S MOOD (12a) Riverside RLP12-235

PRESTIGE ALL STARS—THE CATS

Idrees Sulieman (t), John Coltrane (ts), Tommy Flanagan (p), Kenny Burrell (g), Doug Watkins (b), Louis Hayes (d)

Hackensack, N.J., April 18, 1957

1194	ECLYPSO	(13,13a)	New Jazz NJLP8217
1195	SOLACIUM	(13,13a)	”
1196	MINOR MISHAP	(13,13a)	”
1198	TOMMY'S TIME	(13,13a)	”

Note: Coltrane out on 1197

MAL WALDRON—MAL 2

Bill Hardman (t), Jackie McLean (as), John Coltrane (ts), Mal Waldron (p), Julian Euell (b), Art Taylor (d) *Hackensack, N.J., April 19, 1957*

1199	POTPOURRI	Prestige PRLP7111
1200	J M'S DREAM DOLL	”
1201	DON'T EXPLAIN	”
1202	BLUE CALYPSO	(14) Status ST8316
1203	FALLING IN LOVE WITH LOVE	(14) ”

PRESTIGE ALL STARS

John Coltrane (ts), Pepper Adams, Cecil Payne (bars), Mal Waldron (p), Doug Watkins (b), Art Taylor (d), Teddy Charles (arr) *Hackensack, N.J., April 20, 1957*

1208	DAKAR	(12) Prestige PRLP16-6
1209	MARY'S BLUES	(12) ”
1210	ROUTE 4	(12) ”
1211	VELVET SCENE	(12) ”
1212	WITCHES PIT	(12) ”
1213	CAT WALK	(12) ”

MAL WALDRON—MAL 2

Idrees Sulieman (t), Sahib Shihab (as, bars), John Coltrane (ts), Mal Waldron (p), Julian Euell (b), Ed Thigpen (d) *Hackensack, N.J., May 17, 1957*

1267	THE WAY YOU LOOK TONIGHT	Prestige PRLP7111
1268	FROM THIS MOMENT ON	”
1269	ONE BY ONE	”

PAUL QUINICHETTE/JOHN COLTRANE—CATTIN'

Paul Quinichette (ts) replaces Sulieman and Shihab *Same date*

1270	CATTIN'	(14a) Prestige PRLP7158
1271	ANATOMY	(14a) ”
1272	VODKA	(14a) ”
1273	SUNDAY	(14a) ”
1274	TEA FOR TWO	unissued
1275	EXACTLY LIKE YOU	(14a) Prestige PRLP7158

JOHN COLTRANE

Johnny Splawn (t), John Coltrane (ts), Sahib Shihab (bars), Mal Waldron-1, Red Garland-2 (p), Paul Chambers (b), Al Heath (d)

Hackensack, N.J., May 31, 1957

1292	STRAIGHT STREET -1	(15,15a) Prestige PRLP7105
1293	WHILE MY LADY SLEEPS -1,3	(15,15a) ”
1294	CHRONIC BLUES -1	(15,15a) ”
1295	BAKAI -2	(15,15a) ”
1296	VIOLETS FOR YOUR FURS -2,4	(15,15a) ”
1297	TIME WAS -2,4	(15,15a) Prestige 45-107, PRLP7105
1298	I HEAR A RHAPSODY -2,4	(15,16) Prestige PRLP7188

3-Shihab out, 4-Splawn and Shihab out.

THELONIOUS MONK—MONK'S MUSIC

Ray Copeland (t), Gigi Gryce (as), John Coltrane, Coleman Hawkins (ts), Thelonious Monk (p), Wilbur Ware (b), Art Blakey (d) *NYC, June 26, 1957*

EPISTROPHY/CREPESCULE WITH NELLIE/WELL YOU NEEDN'T/OFF MINOR/ ABIDE WITH ME -1 (12a,17) Riverside RLP12-242
EPISTROPHY (alt. take)/OFF MINOR (alt. take) (12a,18) Jazzland JLP46
BLUES FOR TOMORROW -2 (12a) Riverside RLP12-243
1-Monk, Ware and Blakey out
2-Monk out; recorded June 25, 1957

JOHN COLTRANE—LUSH LIFE

John Coltrane (ts), Earl May (b), Art Taylor (d) *Hackensack, N.J., August 16, 1957*

1334-1	TRANE'S SLOW BLUES	(15,16) Prestige PRLP7188
1334-2	TONI'S DANCE (SLOWTRANE)	(19) Prestige PRLP7378
1335	LIKE SOMEONE IN LOVE	(15,16) Prestige PRLP7188
1336	I LOVE YOU	(15,16) "

JOHN COLTRANE WITH THE RED GARLAND TRIO

John Coltrane (ts), Red Garland (p), Paul Chambers (b), Art Taylor (d)
Hackensack, N.J., August 23, 1957

1337	YOU LEAVE ME BREATHLESS	(20,20a) Prestige PRLP7123
1338	BASS BLUES	(20,20a) "
1339	SOFT LIGHTS AND SWEET MUSIC	(20,20a) "
1340	TRANE-ING IN	(20,20a) Prestige 45-119, PRLP7123
1341	SLOW DANCE	(20,20a) Prestige PRLP7123

SONNY CLARK—SONNY'S CRIB

Donald Byrd (t), Curtis Fuller (tb), John Coltrane (ts), Sonny Clark (p), Paul Chambers (b), Art Taylor (d) *Hackensack, N.J., September 1, 1957*

SONNY'S CRIB/SPEAK LOW/WITH A SONG IN MY HEART/COME RAIN OR COME SHINE/NEWS FOR LULU Blue Note BLP1576

JOHN COLTRANE—BLUE TRAIN

Lee Morgan (t), Curtis Fuller (tb), John Coltrane (ts), Kenny Drew (p), Paul Chambers (b), Philly Joe Jones (d) *Hackensack, N.J., September 15, 1957*

BLUE TRAIN/MOMENT'S NOTICE/LOCOMOTION/I'M OLD FASHIONED/ LAZY BIRD (21) Blue Note BLP1577, BST81577

PRESTIGE ALL STARS—WHEELIN' AND DEALIN'

Frank Wess (f, ts), John Coltrane, Paul Quinichette (ts), Mal Waldron (p), Doug Watkins (b), Art Taylor (d) *Hackensack, N.J., September 20, 1957*

1348	DEALIN'	(14) Prestige PRLP7131
1348 (alt.)	DEALIN' No. 1	(14) Status ST8316
1349	WHEELIN'	(14) Prestige PRLP7131
1349 (alt.)	WHEELIN' No. 1	(14) Status ST8316
1350	ROBBINS' NEST	(14) Prestige PRLP7131
1351	THINGS AIN'T WHAT THEY USED TO BE	(14) Prestige 45-122, PRLP7131

WINNERS' CIRCLE

Donald Byrd (t), Frank Rehak (tb), Gene Quill (as), John Coltrane (ts), Al Cohn (bars), Eddie Costa (p), Freddie Greene (g), Oscar Pettiford (b), Philly Joe Jones-1, Ed Thigpen-2 (d) *NYC, September 1957*

NOT SO SLEEPY-1/LOVE AND THE WEATHER-2,3/IF I'M LUCKY-2,3/TURTLE TALK-2,4/STRICTLY INSTRUMENTAL-2,5 Bethlehem BCP6024

3-Quill and Greene out, 4-Greene out, 5-Costa out

RED GARLAND QUINTET

Donald Byrd (t), John Coltrane (ts), Red Garland (p), George Joyner (Jamil Nasser) (b), Art Taylor (d) *Hackensack, N.J., November 15, 1957*

1392	OUR DELIGHT	(21a) Prestige PRLP7130
1393	THEY CAN'T TAKE THAT AWAY FROM ME	(21a) ”
1394	WOODY'N YOU	(21a) Prestige PRLP7181
1395	I GOT IT BAD	(21a) ”
1396	UNDECIDED	(22) Prestige PRLP7209
1397	SOUL JUNCTION	(21a) Prestige PRLP7181
1398	WHAT IS THERE TO SAY	(22) Prestige PRLP7209
1399	BIRKS' WORKS	(21a) Prestige PRLP7181
1400	HALLELUJAH	(21a) ”
1401	ALL MORNING LONG	(21a) Prestige PRLP7130

Hackensack, N.J., December 13, 1957

1405	BILLIE'S BOUNCE	(22) Prestige PRLP7229
1406	SOLITUDE	(22) Prestige PRLP7209
1407	TWO BASS HIT	(22) ”
1408	SOFT WINDS	(22) ”
1409	LAZY MAE	(22) Prestige PRLP7229

RAY DRAPER—FEATURING JOHN COLTRANE

Ray Draper (tu), John Coltrane (ts), Gil Coggins (p), Spanky DeBrest (b), Larry Ritchie (d) *Hackensack, N.J., December 20, 1957*

1410	UNDER PARIS SKIES	(22a) New Jazz NJLP8228
1411	CLIFFORD'S KAPPA	(22a) ”
1412	FILIDE	(22a) ”
1413	TWO SONS	(22a) ”
1414	PAUL'S PAL	(22a) ”
1415	I HADN'T ANYONE TILL YOU	(22a) ”

Note: Coltrane out on remaining (unissued) track from this session

ART BLAKEY BIG BAND
Donald Byrd, Idrees Sulieman, Bill Hardman, Ray Copeland (t), Melba Liston, Frank Rehak, Jimmy Cleveland (tb), Sahib Shihab, Bill Graham (as), Al Cohn, John Coltrane (ts), Bill Slapin (bars), Walter Bishop (p), Wendell Marshall (b), Art Blakey (d) *NYC, December 1957*

MIDRIFF/AIN'T LIFE GRAND/TIPPIN' -1/PRISTINE -1/EL TORO VALIENTE/THE KISS OF NO RETURN/LATE DATE/THE OUTER WORLD
(22) Bethlehem BCP6027

1-Byrd, Coltrane, Bishop, Marshall and Blakey only

THELONIOUS MONK—THELONIOUS MONK AND JOHN COLTRANE
John Coltrane (ts), Thelonious Monk (p), Wilbur Ware (b), Shadow Wilson (d)
NYC, c. 1957-58

NUTTY/RUBY, MY DEAR/TRINKLE TINKLE (12a, 18) Jazzland JLPS946

GENE AMMONS AND HIS ALL STARS
Jerome Richardson (f), John Coltrane (as), Gene Ammons, Paul Quinichette (ts), Pepper Adams (bars), Mal Waldron (p, arr), George Joyner (Jamil Nasser) (b), Art Taylor (d) *Hackensack, N.J., January 3, 1958*

1426	AMMON JOY	(23) Prestige PRLP7201
1427	GROOVE BLUES	(23) "
1428	THE REAL McCOY	(23) Prestige PRLP7132
1430	IT MIGHT AS WELL BE SPRING -1	(23) Prestige PRLP7201

1-Richardson, Quinichette and Adams out

Note: Coltrane out on remainder

JOHN COLTRANE
Donald Byrd (t), John Coltrane (ts), Red Garland (p), Paul Chambers (b), Louis Hayes (d) *Hackensack, N.J., January 10, 1958*

1434	LUSH LIFE	(15,16) Prestige PRLP7188
1435	THE BELIEVER	(24) Prestige PRLP7292
1436	NAKATINI SERENADE	(24) "
1437	COME RAIN OR COME SHINE	(19) Prestige PRLP7378
1438	LOVER	(19) "

JOHN COLTRANE WITH THE RED GARLAND TRIO—SOULTRANE
John Coltrane (ts), Red Garland (p), Paul Chambers (b), Art Taylor (d)
Hackensack, N.J., February 7, 1958

1460	RUSSIAN LULLABY	(20,25) Prestige PRLP7142
1461	THEME FOR ERNIE	(20,25) "
1462	YOU SAY YOU CARE	(20,25) "
1463	GOOD BAIT	(20,25) Prestige 45-139, PRLP7142
1464	I WANT TO TALK ABOUT YOU	(20,25) Prestige PRLP7142

KENNY BURRELL/JOHN COLTRANE

John Coltrane (ts), Tommy Flanagan (p), Kenny Burrell (g), Paul Chambers (b), Jimmy Cobb (d) *Hackensack, N.J., March 7, 1958*

1476 LYRESTO (13) New Jazz NJ8276
1477 WHY WAS I BORN? -1 (13) ”
1478 FREIGHT TRAIN (13) ”
1479 I NEVER KNEW (13) ”
1480 BIG PAUL (13) ”
1-Coltrane and Burrell only on this track

WILBUR HARDEN—WEST42ND STREET

Wilbur Harden (flh), John Coltrane (ts), Tommy Flanagan (p), Doug Watkins (b), Louis Hayes (d) *Hackensack, N.J., March 13, 1958*

WELLS FARGO ≠1/E.F.F.P.H./RHODOMAGNETICS ≠2/SNUFFY/WEST 42ND STREET (25a)Savoy MG12127
WELLS FARGO ≠2/COUNT DOWN ≠1/COUNT DOWN ≠2/RHODOMAGNETICS ≠1 (25a) Savoy SJL2203

Note: Harden's COUNT DOWN is not related to the Coltrane tune recorded May 5, 1959

JOHN COLTRANE WITH THE RED GARLAND TRIO—SETTIN' THE PACE

John Coltrane (ts), Red Garland (p), Paul Chambers (b), Jimmy Cobb (d) *Hackensack, N.J., March 26, 1958*

1488 RISE AND SHINE (19,26) Prestige PRLP7213
1489 I SEE YOUR FACE BEFORE ME (19,26) ”
1490 IF THERE IS SOMEONE LOVELIER THAN YOU (19,26) ”
1491 LITTLE MELONAE (19,26) ”
1492 BY THE NUMBERS (19) Prestige PR7378

MILES DAVIS—MILESTONES

Miles Davis (t), Cannonball Adderley (as), John Coltrane (ts), Red Garland (p) Paul Chambers (b), Philly Joe Jones (d) *NYC, April 2, 1958*

CO60199 TWO BASS HIT (27) Columbia CL1193
CO60201 STRAIGHT NO CHASER (27) ”
CO60202 MILESTONES (MILES) -1 (27) Columbia B11931, CL1193

NYC, April 3, 1958

CO60203 DR. JEKYLL (i.e. DR. JACKYL) (27) Columbia B11931, CL1193
CO60204 SID'S AHEAD (i.e. WEIRDO) -2 (27) Columbia CL1193
1-Davis (flh); 2-Davis also plays p, replacing Garland

Note: Coltrane out on CO60200

WILBUR HARDEN—TANGANYIKA STRUT
Wilbur Harden (flh), Curtis Fuller (tb), John Coltrane (ts), Howard Williams (p), Alvin Jackson (b), Art Taylor (d) *Hackensack, N.J., May 13, 1958*

	B.J./ANEDAC/ONCE IN A WHILE	(28) Savoy MG12136
	B.J. (alt. take)	(29) Savoy SJL1115

MILES DAVIS
As for April 2 except Adderley out, Bill Evans (p) replaces Garland
Cafe Bohemia, NYC, prob. May 17, 1958

	BYE BYE BLACKBIRD/WALKIN' (ROLLIN' AND BLOWIN')/FOUR (FOUR PLUS ONE MORE)	Chakra CH100MD

JOHN COLTRANE—BLACK PEARLS
Donald Byrd (t), John Coltrane (ts), Red Garland (p), Paul Chambers (b), Jimmy Cobb (d) *Hackensack, N.J., May 23, 1958*

1513	BLACK PEARLS	(24) Prestige PR7316
1514	LOVER COME BACK TO ME	(24) "
1515	SWEET SAPPHIRE BLUES	(24) "

MILES DAVIS—JAZZ TRACK
As for May 17 except Jimmy Cobb (d) replaces Jones, Adderley returns
NYC, May 26, 1958

CO61165	ON GREEN DOLPHIN STREET	(7) Columbia CL1268
CO61166	FRAN-DANCE	(7) "
CO61167	STELLA BY STARLIGHT -1	(7) "
CO61168	LOVE FOR SALE	Columbia PG33402

1-Adderley out on this track

MICHEL LEGRAND—LEGRAND JAZZ
Miles Davis (t), Herbie Mann (f), Phil Woods (as), John Coltrane (ts), Jerome Richardson (bars, cl), Eddie Costa (vib), Bill Evans (p), Paul Chambers (b), Kenny Dennis (d), Betty Glamann (harp), Michel Legrand (arr, cond)
NYC, June 25, 1958

CO61067	WILD MAN BLUES	Columbia CL1250
CO61068	'ROUND MIDNIGHT	"
CO61069	JITTERBURG WALTZ	"

Note: Coltrane out on remaining track

WILBUR HARDEN—DIAL AFRICA
As for May 13 except Tommy Flanagan (p) replaces Williams
Hackensack, N.J., June 29, 1958

	DIAL AFRICA/OOMBA	(28) Savoy MG12131
	DIAL AFRICA (alt. take)	(29) Savoy SJL1115
	GOLD COAST	(29) Savoy MG12131
	TANGANYIKA STRUT	(29) Savoy MG12136

MILES DAVIS—MILES AT NEWPORT

As for May 26 — *Freebody Park, Newport, R.I., July 3, 1958*

CO81844	AH-LEU-CHA	(30)	Columbia CL2178, CS8978
CO81845	STRAIGHT NO CHASER	(30)	" "
CO81846	FRAN-DANCE	(30)	" "
CO81847	TWO BASS HIT	(30)	" "
	BYE BYE BLACKBIRD	(30a)	FDC FDC1024
	THE THEME		"

JOHN COLTRANE

As for May 23 except Wilbur Harden (flh) replaces Byrd

Hackensack, N.J., July 11, 1958

1541	SPRING IS HERE	(31)	Prestige PR7243
1542	INVITATION	(31)	"
1543	I'M A DREAMER AREN'T WE ALL	(31)	Prestige PR7353
1544	LOVE THY NEIGHBOUR	(31)	Prestige PR7268
1545	DON'T TAKE YOUR LOVE AWAY	(31)	Prestige PR7243
1546	STARDUST	(31)	Prestige PR7268
1547	MY IDEAL	(31)	Prestige PR7353
1548	I'LL GET BY	(31)	Prestige PR7243

MILES DAVIS—JAZZ AT THE PLAZA VOL. 1

As for May 26 — *Plaza Hotel, NYC, September 9, 1958*

CO93314	IF I WERE A BELL -1	(31a)	Columbia PC32470
CO93317	OLEO	(31a)	"
	STRAIGHT NO CHASER/THE THEME	(31a)	"

1-Adderley out

Note: Coltrane out on remaining track

GEORGE RUSSELL—NEW YORK N.Y.

Ernie Royal, Doc Severinsen, Art Farmer (t), Bob Brookmeyer, Frank Rehak, Tom Mitchell (tb), Hal McKusick (as), John Coltrane (ts), Sol Schlinger (bars), Bill Evans (p), Barry Galbraith (g), Milt Hinton (b), Charlie Persip (d), Jon Hendricks (narr), George Russell (arr, cond) — *NYC, September 12, 1958*

105626 MANHATTAN — Decca DL9216, DLS79216

CECIL TAYLOR—HARD DRIVING JAZZ

Kenny Dorham (t), 'Blue Train' (John Coltrane) (ts), Cecil Taylor (p), Chuck Israels (b), Louis Hayes (d) — *NYC, October 13, 1958*

SHIFTING DOWN/LIKE SOMEONE IN LOVE/JUST FRIENDS/DOUBLE CLUTCHING — (32) United Artists UAL4014, UAS5014

CARAVAN — unissued

RAY DRAPER—TUBA JAZZ

Ray Draper (tu), John Coltrane (ts), John Mayer (p), Spanky DeBrest (b), Larry Ritchie (d) — *NYC, late 1958*

ESSIL'S DANCE/DOXY/I TALK TO THE TREES/YESTERDAYS/OLEO/ANGEL EYES — (32a) Jubilee JLP1090

JOHN COLTRANE

Freddie Hubbard (t-1), John Coltrane (ts), Red Garland (p), Paul Chambers (b), Art Taylor-2, Jimmy Cobb-3 (d) *Hackensack, N.J., December 26, 1958*

1696	DO I LOVE YOU BECAUSE YOU'RE BEAUTIFUL -1,2	(24) Prestige PR7292
1697	THEN I'LL BE TIRED OF YOU -1,2	(14a) Prestige PR7268
1698	SOMETHING I DREAMED LAST NIGHT -3	(14a) Prestige PR7353
1699	BAHIA -2	(14a) "
1700	GOLDSBORO EXPRESS -2,4	(14a) "
1701	TIME AFTER TIME -3	(14a) Prestige PR7268
	4-Garland out on this track	

JOHN COLTRANE/MILT JACKSON—BAGS AND TRANE

John Coltrane (ts), Milt Jackson (vib), Hank Jones (p), Paul Chambers (b), Connie Kay (d) *NYC, January 15, 1959*

3300	STAIRWAY TO THE STARS	Atlantic SD1553
3301	THE LATE, LATE BLUES	Atlantic LP/SD1368
3302	BAGS AND TRANE	"
3303	THREE LITTLE WORDS	"
3304	THE NIGHT WE CALLED IT A DAY	"
3305	BE-BOP	"
3306	BLUES LEGACY	Atlantic SD1553
3307	CENTERPIECE	"

CANNONBALL ADDERLEY—IN CHICAGO

Cannonball Adderley (as), John Coltrane (ts), Wynton Kelly (p), Paul Chambers (b), Jimmy Cobb (d) *Chicago, February 3, 1959*

18094	GRAND CENTRAL	(33) Mercury MG20449
18095	THE SLEEPER	(33) "
18096	WABASH	(33) "
18097	WEAVER OF DREAMS -1	(33) "
18098	LIMEHOUSE BLUES	(33) "
	1-Adderley out	

Note: Coltrane out on remaining track

MILES DAVIS—KIND OF BLUE

Miles Davis (t), Cannonball Adderley (as), John Coltrane (ts), Wynton Kelly-1, Bill Evans-2 (p), Paul Chambers (b), Jimmy Cobb (d) *NYC, March 2, 1959*

CO62290	FREDDIE FREELOADER -1	(34) Columbia CL1355, CS8163
CO62291	SO WHAT -2	(34) " "
CO62292	BLUE IN GREEN -2,3	(34) " "
	3-Adderley out	

JOHN COLTRANE—ALTERNATE TAKES

John Coltrane (ts), Cedar Walton (p), Paul Chambers (b), Lex Humphries (d) *NYC, April 1, 1959*

3420	GIANT STEPS	(34a) Atlantic SD1668
3421	NAIMA	(34a) "
3422	LIKE SONNY	(34a) "

MILES DAVIS QUINTET

Miles Davis (t), John Coltrane (ts), Wynton Kelly (p), Paul Chambers (b), Jimmy Cobb (d) WITH GIL EVANS AND HIS ORCHESTRA: Ernie Royal, Louis Mucci, Clyde Reasinger, Johnny Coles, Emmett Berry (t), Frank Rehak, Jimmy Cleveland, Bill Elton (tb), Rod Levitt (btb), Julius Watkins, Bob Northern (fr-h), Bill Barber (tu), Romeo Penque, Eddie Caine (woodwinds), Danny Bank (bcl), unknown harp, Gil Evans (arr, cond) *NYC, April 2, 1959*

SO WHAT-1/THE DUKE-2/BLUES FOR PABLO-2/NEW RUMBA-2 Ozone 18

1-Quintet plus 3 tb only, 2-Coltrane plays as and Kelly out

MILES DAVIS—KIND OF BLUE

As for May 26, 1958 *NYC, April 22, 1959*

CO62293	FLAMENCO SKETCHES	(34) Columbia CL1355, CS8163
CO62294	ALL BLUES	(34) ,, ,,

JOHN COLTRANE—GIANT STEPS

John Coltrane (ts), Tommy Flanagan (p), Paul Chambers (b), Art Taylor (d)

NYC, May 4, 1959

3469	COUSIN MARY	(35) Atlantic 45-5003, LP/SD1311
3469 (alt.)	COUSIN MARY	(34a) Atlantic SD1668
3462	SPIRAL	(35) Atlantic LP/SD1311
3463	SWEET SIOUX	unissued

NYC, May 5, 1959

3464	COUNTDOWN	(35) Atlantic LP/SD1311
3464 (alt.)	COUNTDOWN	(34a) Atlantic SD1668
3465	NAIMA	unissued
3466	SYEEDA'S SONG FLUTE	(35) Atlantic LP/SD1311
3466 (alt.)	SYEEDA'S SONG FLUTE	(34a) Atlantic SD1668
3467	MR. P.C.	(35) Atlantic LP/SD1311
3468	GIANT STEPS	(35) ,,

JOHN COLTRANE—COLTRANE JAZZ

Wynton Kelly (p), Jimmy Cobb (d) replace Flanagan and Taylor

NYC, November 24, 1959

3883	FIFTH HOUSE	unissued
3884	SOME OTHER BLUES	,,
3885	I'LL WAIT AND PRAY	Atlantic LP/SD1354
3885 (alt.)	I'LL WAIT AND PRAY	(34a) Atlantic SD1668
3886	LITTLE OLD LADY	Atlantic LP/SD1354

NYC, December 2, 1959

3891	LIKE SONNY	Atlantic LP/SD1354
3892	HARMONIQUE	,,
3893	THE NIGHT HAS A THOUSAND EYES	unissued
3894	EQUINOX	,,
3895	MY SHINING HOUR	Atlantic LP/SD1354

3896	NAIMA	(35) Atlantic 45-5003, LP/SD1311
3897	SOME OTHER BLUES	Atlantic LP/SD1354
3898	FIFTH HOUSE	”

MILES DAVIS QUINTET

As for April 22, 1959 — *Konserthuset, Stockholm, March 22, 1960*

SO WHAT/ON GREEN DOLPHIN STREET/ALL BLUES/THE THEME/
SO WHAT/FRAN-DANCE/WALKIN'/THE THEME (35a) Dragon DRLP90/91

Kurhaus, Scheveningen, April 9, 1960

ON GREEN DOLPHIN STREET/SO WHAT/'ROUND MIDNIGHT/WALKIN'/THE
THEME (35b) Unique Jazz UJ19

JOHN COLTRANE/DON CHERRY—THE AVANT-GARDE

Don Cherry (t), John Coltrane (ss-1, ts-2), Charlie Haden (b), Ed Blackwell (d)

NYC, June 28, 1960

4662	CHERRYCO -2	(36) Atlantic SD1451
4663	THE BLESSING -1	(36) ”
4664	THE INVISIBLE	unissued

Percy Heath (b) replaces Haden — *NYC, July 8, 1960*

4688	FOCUS ON SANITY -2	(36) Atlantic SD1451
4689	THE BLESSING	unissued
4690	THE INVISIBLE -2	(36) Atlantic SD1451
4691	BEMSHA SWING -2	(36) ”

JOHN COLTRANE QUARTET

John Coltrane (ss-1, ts-2), McCoy Tyner (p), Steve Davis (b), Billy Higgins (d)

NYC, c. September 1960

EXOTICA-2/MR. DAY (ONE AND FOUR)-2/LIKE SONNY-2 Roulette R52094

Elvin Jones (d) replaces Higgins — *NYC, October 21, 1960*

5118	VILLAGE BLUES -2	Atlantic LP/SD1354
5119	EQUINOX	unissued
5120	MY FAVOURITE THINGS -1	(36a) Atlantic LP/SD1361
5121	THE NIGHT HAS A THOUSAND EYES	unissued

NYC, October 24, 1960

5126	CENTRAL PARK WEST -1	Atlantic LP/SD1419
5127	MR. SYMS -1	(37) Atlantic LP/SD1382
5128	EXOTICA (UNTITLED ORIGINAL) -1	Atlantic SD1553
5129	SUMMERTIME -2	(36a) Atlantic LP/SD1361
5130 (alt.)	BODY AND SOUL -2	(34a) Atlantic SD1668
5130	BODY AND SOUL -2	Atlantic LP/SD1419
5133	MR. KNIGHT -2	(37) Atlantic LP/SD1382
5134	BLUES TO ELVIN -2	(37) ”

5125	MR. DAY -2	(37)	”
5136	BLUES TO YOU -2,3	(37)	”
5137	BLUES TO BECHET -1,3	(37)	”
5138	SATELLITE -2		Atlantic LP/SD1419

NYC, October 26, 1960

5139	EV'RY TIME WE SAY GOODBYE -1	(36a)	Atlantic LP/SD1361
5140	26-2 -1,2		Atlantic SD1553
5141	BUT NOT FOR ME -2	(36a)	Atlantic LP/SD1361
5142	LIBERIA -2		Atlantic LP/SD1419
5143	THE NIGHT HAS A THOUSAND EYES -2		”
5144	EQUINOX -2		”

3-Tyner out

Note: Coltrane out on 5131 and 5132 (Tyner, Davis and Jones only)

MILES DAVIS—SOMEDAY MY PRINCE WILL COME

Miles Davis (t), Hank Mobley, John Coltrane (ts), Wynton Kelly (p), Paul Chambers (b), Jimmy Cobb (d) *NYC, March 20, 1961*

CO66500 SOME DAY MY PRINCE WILL COME (37a) Columbia CL1656

NYC, March 21, 1961

CO66505 TEO -1 (37a) Columbia CL1656

1-Mobley out

Note: Coltrane out on other tracks from these sessions

JOHN COLTRANE QUARTET (sic)**—AFRICA/BRASS**

Booker Little, Freddie Hubbard (t), Charles Greenlee (Harnifan Majid), Julian Priester (euph), Jimmy Buffington, Julius Watkins, Donald Corrado, Bob Northern, Robert Swisshel (fr-h), John Coltrane (ss, ts), Eric Dolphy (as, f, bcl, arr-1), Pat Patrick, Garvin Bushell (reeds), McCoy Tyner (p), Reggie Workman-2, Paul Chambers-3 (b), Elvin Jones (d), Cal Massey (arr-4), Romulus Franceschini (cond-5) *Englewood Cliffs, N.J., May 23, 1961*

GREENSLEEVES -1,2 (38) Impulse AS-6

GREENSLEEVES (alt. take) -1,2/SONG OF THE UNDERGROUND RAILROAD -2 (39) Impulse AS9273

THE DAMNED DON'T CRY -2,4,5/AFRICA (alt take) -1,2,3 Impulse AS9361/2

JOHN COLTRANE—OLÉ

Freddie Hubbard (t), John Coltrane (ss-1, ts-2), 'George Lane' (Eric Dolphy) (as-3, f-4), McCoy Tyner (p), Art Davis-5, Reggie Workman-6 (b), Elvin Jones (d)

NYC, May 25, 1961

5556	VENGA VALLEJO (OLÉ) -1,4,5,6	(40)	Atlantic LP/SD1373
5557	DAHOMEY DANCE -2,3,5,6	(40)	”
5558	AISHA -2,4,6	(40)	”
5559	TO HER LADYSHIP -1,3,5		Atlantic SD1553

JOHN COLTRANE QUARTET (sic)

As for May 23 except Hubbard, Greenlee, Priester, Buffington, Bushell, Chambers, Massey, Franceschini out; Britt Woodman (tb), Carl Bowman (euph), Bill Barber (tu), Art Davis (b-6) added *Englewood Cliffs, N.J., June 7, 1961*

	AFRICA (alt. take) -1,2,6	(39) Impulse AS9273
	AFRICA -1,2,6/BLUES MINOR -2	(38) Impulse AS-6

JOHN COLTRANE

John Coltrane (ss, ts), Eric Dolphy (as, f, bcl), Garvin Bushell (cbsn-1), Ahmed Abdul-Malik (oud-2), McCoy Tyner (p), Reggie Workman-3, Jimmy Garrison-4 (b), Elvin Jones *Village Vanguard, NYC, November 1, 1961*

	INDIA -2,3,4	rejected
	CHASIN' THE TRANE (alt. take) -3,5	(40a) Impulse AS9325
	IMPRESSIONS (alt. take) -4	Impulse AS9361/2
	SPIRITUAL (alt. take) -3	(40a) Impulse AS9325
10570	MILES' MODE -3	Impulse AS9361/2
	NAIMA -3	"
10571	BRASILIA (UNTITLED ORIGINAL) -3	(40a) Impulse AS9325

Village Vanguard, NYC, November 2, 1961

	CHASIN' ANOTHER TRANE 3,5,7	Impulse AS9361/2
10572	SOFTLY AS IN A MORNING SUNRISE -3,6	(41) Impulse AS-10
10576	CHASIN' THE TRANE -4,5,6	(41) "
	INDIA -1,2,3,4	rejected
	SPIRITUAL -1,3	"
10573	GREENSLEEVES -3	(40a) Impulse AS9352
	IMPRESSIONS -4	Impulse AS9361/2

Village Vanguard, NYC, November 3, 1961

10557	SPIRITUAL -3,6	(41) Impulse AS-10
	NAIMA -3	rejected
10575	IMPRESSIONS -4,6	(42) Impulse AS-42
10556	INDIA -3,4	(42) "
	GREENSLEEVES -3,6	Impulse AS9361/2
	MILES' MODE -3,4	rejected

Village Vanguard, NYC, November 5, 1961

	INDIA -1,2,3,4	(40a) Impulse AS9325
	SPIRITUAL -1,3	(40a) "

5-Tyner out, 6-Dolphy out, 7-Roy Haynes (d) replaces Jones

Note: Contrary to information on AS9325, Bushell plays only cbsn and not oboe

John Coltrane (ss-1, ts-2), Eric Dolphy (as-3, f-4, bcl-5), McCoy Tyner (p), Reggie Workman (b), Elvin Jones (d) *Konserthuset, Stockholm, November 23, 1961*

MY FAVOURITE THINGS -1,4/IMPRESSIONS-2,3/NAIMA* -2,5

(43) Historical Performance LP1

MY FAVOURITE THINGS -1,4/BLUE TRAIN -2,3/NAIMA -2,5/IMPRESSIONS -2,3
(44) Historical Performance LP5

Note: Material drawn from two different concerts, probably on the same day; both albums originally issued as by ERIC DOLPHY QUINTET FEATURING BLUE TRANE

Baden-Baden, November 26, 1961

MY FAVOURITE THINGS/EV'RY TIME WE SAY GOODBYE/
IMPRESSIONS/UNKNOWN TITLE — Jazz Connoisseur JC112

Jimmy Garrison (b) replaces Workman — *NYC, December 21, 1961*

10669	GREENSLEEVES -1	Impulse 203
10670	IT'S EASY TO REMEMBER -2	(45) Impulse 203, AS-32

Birdland, NYC, February 10, 1962

MR. P.C. -2,3/MILES' MODE -2,3/MY FAVOURITE THINGS -1,4
(46, 46a) Ozone 10

Dolphy out — *Englewood Cliffs, N.J., April 11, 1962*

10873	SOUL EYES	unissued
10874	THE INCHWORM -1	(47) Impulse AS-21
10875	BIG NICK -1	(47) Impulse AS-99

Englewood Cliffs, N.J., April 12, 1962

10876	SOUL EYES	unissued
10877	EXCERPT	,,
10878	BODY AND SOUL	,,
10879	NEPTUNE	,,

Birdland, NYC, June 2, 1962

MY FAVOURITE THINGS -1	Alto 724
BODY AND SOUL -2	(46) ,,

Englewood Cliffs, N.J., June 19, 1962

10979	NOT YET	unissued
10980	OUT OF THIS WORLD -2	(47) Impulse AS-21
10981	SOUL EYES -2	(47) ,,
10982	EXCERPT	unissued

Englewood Cliffs, N.J., June 21, 1962

10983	NOT YET	unissued
10984	MILES' MODE -2	(47) Impulse AS-21
10985	TWO, THREE, FOUR	unissued
10986	EXCERPT	,,

Englewood Cliffs, N.J., June 29, 1962

10992	TUNJI -2	(47) Impulse AS-21
10993	OUT OF THIS WORLD	unissued
10994	UP 'GAINST THE WALL	,,

Englewood Cliffs, N.J., September 18, 1962

11092	NANCY (WITH THE LAUGHING FACE) -2	(45) Impulse 212, AS-32
11093	WHAT'S NEW -2	(45) " "
11094	UP 'GAINST THE WALL -2,3	(42) Impulse AS-42
	3-Tyner out on this track	

DUKE ELLINGTON AND JOHN COLTRANE

John Coltrane (ss-1, ts-2), Duke Ellington (p), Jimmy Garrison-3, Aaron Bell-4 (b), Elvin Jones-5, Sam Woodyard-6 (d) *Englewood Cliffs, N.J., September 26, 1962*

11114	STEVIE -2,4,6	(48) Impulse AS-30
11115	IN A SENTIMENTAL MOOD -2,4,5	(48) "
11116	ANGELICA -2,3,5	(48) "
11117	BIG NICK -1,3,5	(48) "
11118	MY LITTLE BROWN BOOK -2,4,6	(48) "
11119	THE FEELING OF JAZZ -2,4,6	(48) "
11120	TAKE THE COLTRANE -2,3,5	(48) "

JOHN COLTRANE—BALLADS

As for September 18 *Englewood Cliffs, N.J., November 13, 1962*

11161	TOO YOUNG TO GO STEADY -2	(45) Impulse AS-32
11162	ALL OR NOTHING AT ALL -2	(45) "
11163	I WISH I KNEW -2	(45) "
11164	THEY SAY IT'S WONDERFUL	unissued
11165	YOU DON'T KNOW WHAT LOVE IS -2	(45) Impulse AS-32
11166	SAY IT OVER AND OVER AGAIN -2	(45) "

Olympia, Paris, November 17, 1962

MR. P.C./THE INCHWORM (48a) Pablo 2308.217

EV'RY TIME WE SAY GOODBYE (48a, 54) "

Konserthuset, Stockholm, November 19, 1962

MR. P.C./BYE BYE BLACKBIRD/THE INCHWORM

Historical Performance LP2

NAIMA/TRANEING IN/IMPRESSIONS Historical Performance LP3

THE INCHWORM/IMPRESSIONS/MY FAVOURITE THINGS

(49) Duke D1016

Note: Material drawn from two concerts; first two LPs issued as by BLUE TRANE

poss. Stefaniensaal, Graz, November 28, 1962

THE INCHWORM/EV'RY TIME WE SAY GOODBYE/IMPRESSIONS

(50) Unique Jazz UJ32

Birdland, NYC, February 23, 1963

I WANT TO TALK ABOUT YOU -2/ONE UP AND ONE DOWN -2/THE INCHWORM* -1 Ozone 21, Session 115

Birdland, NYC, March 2, 1963

MR. P.C. -2/MY FAVOURITE THINGS -1 Alto 724

Englewood Cliffs, N.J., March 6, 1963

11382 VILIA -1 — Impulse AS9101
11383 UNTITLED ORIGINAL — unissued
11384 NATURE BOY — ,,
11385 UNTITLED ORIGINAL — ,,
11386 UNTITLED ORIGINAL — ,,
11387 UNTITLED ORIGINAL — ,,
11388 SLOW BLUES ORIGINAL — ,,

Johnny Hartman (vcl-3) added — *Englewood Cliffs, N.J., March 7, 1963*

11400 THEY SAY IT'S WONDERFUL -2,3 — Impulse AS-40
11401 LUSH LIFE -2,3 — ,,
11402 MY ONE AND ONLY LOVE -2,3 — ,,
11403 AUTUMN SERENADE -2,3 — ,,
11404 DEDICATED TO YOU -1,3 — ,,
11405 AFRO-BLUE — unissued
11406 YOU ARE TOO BEAUTIFUL -2,3 — Impulse AS-40

Roy Haynes (d) replaces Jones — *Englewood Cliffs, N.J., April 29, 1963*

11466 AFTER THE RAIN -2 — (42) Impulse AS-42
11467 ALL THE THINGS YOU ARE — unissued
11468 DEAR OLD STOCKHOLM -2 — Impulse AS-100

Freebody Park, Newport, R.I., July 7, 1963

(90966) I WANT TO TALK ABOUT YOU -2 — Impulse AS9161
(90965) MY FAVOURITE THINGS -2,1 — ,,
IMPRESSIONS -2 — Impulse IZ 9346-2

Elvin Jones (d) replaces Haynes — *Birdland, NYC, October 8, 1963*

90001 THE PROMISE -1 — (51) Impulse AS-50
90002 AFRO-BLUE -1 — (51) ,,
90003 I WANT TO TALK ABOUT YOU -2 — (51) ,,
90004 MR. P.C. — unissued
90005 ROCKIN' — ,,

Konserthuset, Stockholm, October 22, 1963

TRANEING IN — (52) Historical Performance LP6
MR. P.C.* — (52) ,,
SPIRITUAL — (52, 53) ,,
I WANT TO TALK ABOUT YOU — (52) ,,
IMPRESSIONS — (43, 53) Historical Performance LP1

Liederhalle, Stuttgart, November 4, 1963

AFRO-BLUE/THE PROMISE/I WANT TO TALK ABOUT YOU/
MY FAVOURITE THINGS — Jazz Galore 1001

from European concerts, prob. 1962 and 1963

	LONNIE'S LAMENT/NAIMA/MY FAVOURITE THINGS/COUSIN MARY/I WANT TO TALK ABOUT YOU	(53) Pablo 2620.101
	AFRO-BLUE/CHASIN' THE TRANE	(53,54) Pablo 2620.101
	I WANT TO TALK ABOUT YOU/NAIMA/MR. P.C.	(55) Pablo 2308.222
	THE PROMISE	(55,54) Pablo 2308.222
	TRANEING IN	(56) Pablo 2308.227
	BYE BYE BLACKBIRD	(56,54) Pablo 2308.227

NYC, November 18, 1963

90017	YOUR LADY -1	(51) Impulse AS-50
90018	ALABAMA -2	(51) "

Note: Most issues of 90018 contain the incomplete Take 4 as well as Take 5, which lasts 2'40" and was intended for issue alone

KQED-TV, San Fransisco, early 1964

	AFRO-BLUE -1/ALABAMA -2/IMPRESSIONS* -1	Session 126

Englewood Cliffs, N.J., April 27, 1964

90081	CRESCENT	unissued
90082	LONNIE'S LAMENT -2	(57) Impulse AS-66
90083	THE DRUM THING -2	(57) "
90084	WISE ONE -2	(57) "
90085	BESSIE'S BLUES	unissued
90086	SONG OF PRAISE	"

Englewood Cliffs, N.J., June 1, 1964

90127	CRESCENT -2	(57) Impulse AS-66
90128	BESSIE'S BLUES -2	(57) "

Englewood Cliffs, N.J., December 9, 1964

90243	A LOVE SUPREME: ACKNOWLEDGEMENT -2	(58) Impulse AS-77
90244	A LOVE SUPREME: RESOLUTION -2	(58) "
90245	A LOVE SUPREME: PURSUANCE and PSALM -2	(58) "

Archie Shepp (ts), Art Davis (b) added — *Englewood Cliffs, N.J., December 10, 1964*

90246	A LOVE SUPREME (4 parts)	unissued

Shepp out — *Englewood Cliffs, N.J., February 17, 1965*

90253	NATURE BOY -2	Impulse IZ 9345-2
90254	FEELING GOOD	unissued
90255	CHIM CHIM CHEREE	"

Englewood Cliffs, N.J., February 18, 1965

90256	NATURE BOY -2	Impulse AS-85
90257	FEELING GOOD -2	Impulse IZ 9345-2

Davis out *Half Note, NYC, March 19, 1965*

CHIM CHIM CHEREE-1/IMPRESSIONS-2 J For Jazz JFJ 800

Village Gate, NYC, March 28, 1965

90374 NATURE BOY -2 Impulse AS-90

Half Note, NYC, April 2, 1965

UNKNOWN TITLE (CREATION) Blue Parrot AR700

Half Note, NYC, May 7, 1965

SONG OF PRAISE Ozone 21

Englewood Cliffs, N.J., May 17, 1965

90305	CHIM CHIM CHEREE -1	Impulse AS-85
90306	BRASILIA -2	"
90307	SONG OF PRAISE -2	"

Roy Haynes (d) replaces Jones *Englewood Cliffs, N.J., May 26, 1965*

90308	AFTER THE CRESCENT-2	Impulse IZ 9346-2
90309	DEAR LORD -2	(59) Impulse AS9195
90310	ONE DOWN, ONE UP	Impulse IZ 9346-2
90311	WELCOME	unissued

Elvin Jones (d) replaces Haynes *Englewood Cliffs, N.J., June 10, 1965*

90312	WELCOME -2	(60) Impulse AS9106
90313	UNKNOWN TITLE (THE LAST BLUES)	unissued
90314	UNTITLED ORIGINAL-2	Impulse IZ 9345-2
90315	TRANSITION -2	(59) Impulse AS9195
90316	SUITE (5 parts) -2	(59) "

Englewood Cliffs, N.J., June 16, 1965

90317	LIVING SPACE -1,3	Impulse AS9225
90318	DUSK DAWN-2	Impulse IZ 9345-2
90319	VIGIL -2	(60) Impulse AS9106
90320	UNTITLED ORIGINAL-2	Impulse IZ 9345-2

3-Alice Coltrane (harp, tambour), Joan Chapman (tambour), Oran Coltrane (bells), four vlns, two vlas, two cel and —posthumously— John Coltrane (ss) overdubbed April 16 & 17, 1972

Note: 90310 and (from July 2) 90350 are not the same tune as ONE UP AND ONE DOWN (recorded February 23, 1963)

JOHN COLTRANE – ASCENSION

Freddie Hubbard, Dewey Johnson (t), John Tchicai, Marion Brown (as), John Coltrane, Archie Shepp, Pharaoh Sanders (ts), McCoy Tyner (p), Jimmy Garrison, Art Davis (b), Elvin Jones (d) *Englewood Cliffs, N.J., June 28, 1965*

90321/2-1 ASCENSION (take 1) Impulse AS-95

90321/2-2 ASCENSION (take 2) (61) Impulse AS-95

Note: Take 1 was used for earlier issues of AS-95 and initial releases in U.K. and France, take 2 for later copies of AS-95 and most reissues; Marion Brown's book *Reflections* gives the date as July 26, 1965 by which time Coltrane was in France.

JOHN COLTRANE

As for June 16 — *Freebody Park, Newport, R.I., July 2, 1965*

90350	ONE DOWN, ONE UP -2	(62) Impulse AS-94
	MY FAVOURITE THINGS -1	unissued

Pinede Gould, Antibes, July 26, 1965

	A LOVE SUPREME-2	(62a) Ingo 11

Pinede Gould, Antibes, July 27, 1965

	NAIMA -2/IMPRESSIONS -2	(63) Byg YX4001/4002

Salle Pleyel, Paris, July 28, 1965

	AFRO-BLUE -1/IMPRESSIONS -2/ASCENSION (BLUE VALSE)* -1	(63) Byg YX4001/4002

NYC, August 26, 1965

90363	DEARLY BELOVED -2	Impulse AS9211
90364	ATTAINING -2	"
90365	SUNSHIP -2	"
90366	ASCENT -2	"
90367	AMEN -2	"

Englewood Cliffs, N.J., September 2, 1965

90379	LOVE and COMPASSION and JOY -2	Impulse AS9332
90380	CONSEQUENCES and SERENITY -2	"

San Francisco, September 22, 1965

	JOY -3	Impulse AS9225

3-Alice Coltrane (harp, vib), Charlie Haden (b), four vlns, two vlas, two cel overdubbed April 16 & 17, 1972

John Coltrane (ss, ts), Pharaoh Sanders (ts), Donald Garrett (bcl, b), McCoy Tyner (p), Jimmy Garrison (b), Elvin Jones (d)

The Penthouse, Seattle, September 30, 1965

	COSMOS/OUT OF THIS WORLD/EVOLUTION/TAPESTRY IN SOUND -1	(64) Impulse AS 9202-2
	BASS DUET -1/THUMB PIANO PIECE -1/BODY AND SOUL/MY FAVOURITE THINGS	unissued

1-Coltrane out

As for September 30 plus Joe Brazil (f), Coltrane and Sanders also narr

Lynwood, WA, October 1, 1965

90435/6 OM Impulse AS9140

As for September 30 plus Frank Butler (d, perc), Juno Lewis (vcl-2, perc)

Los Angeles, October 14, 1965

90676 KULU SE MAMA -2 (60) Impulse AS9106

90677 SELFLESSNESS Impulse AS9161

As for September 30 except Garrett replaced by Rashied Ali (d)

Englewood Cliffs, N.J., November 23, 1965

90413 THE FATHER AND THE SON AND THE HOLY GHOST and COMPASSION (65) Impulse AS9110

90414 LOVE and SERENITY and CONSEQUENCES (65) "

John Coltrane (ss, ts, bcl), Pharaoh Sanders (ts, f, picc), Alice Coltrane (p), Jimmy Garrison (b), Rashied Ali (d), Ray Appleton (perc)

San Francisco, February 2, 1966

90986 MANIFESTATION Coltrane Recording Corporation AU4590

90987 REVEREND KING "

PEACE ON EARTH -1,2 Impulse AS9225

LEO -1 "

1-Alice Coltrane (org, vib), four vlns, two vlas, two cel and—displacing Garrison—Charlie Haden (b) overdubbed April 16 & 17, 1972; 2-Sanders out

Appleton out *Prob. NYC, April 21, 1966*

90536 DARKNESS unissued

90537 LEAD US ON "

90538 LEO "

90539 PEACE ON EARTH "

Prob. NYC, April 28, 1966

90540 CALL unissued

90541 LEO "

Emanuel Rahim (perc) added *Village Vanguard, NYC, May 28, 1966*

90644 MY FAVOURITE THINGS (66) Impulse AS9124

90645 NAIMA (66) "

Rahim out *Sankei Hall, Tokyo, July 11, 1966*

AFRO-BLUE/PEACE ON EARTH/BASS INTRODUCTION/CRESCENT/LEO Impulse (J) YB8508/8509/8510

Koseinenkin Hall, Tokyo, July 22, 1966

	MEDITATIONS and LEO/PEACE ON EARTH	Impulse AS9246, (J) IMR9036C
	MY FAVOURITE THINGS	Impulse (J) IMR9036C

As July 11 except Coltrane plays ts, f and Sanders f, picc

Prob. Englewood Cliffs, N.J., February 15, 1967

90769	TO BE	(67) Impulse AS9120
90770	OFFERING	(67) "

John Coltrane (ts, bells), Rashied Ali (d) *Englewood Cliffs, N.J., February 22, 1967*

	MARS/VENUS/JUPITER/SATURN	Impulse ASD9277
	LEO/JUPITER VARIATION	Impulse IA 9360

As February 15 except Marion Brown (as) replaces Sanders

Prob. Englewood Cliffs, N.J., February 27, 1967

90774	E MINOR	unissued
90775	HALF STEPS	"

John Coltrane (ts), Alice Coltrane (p), Jimmy Garrison (b) Rashied Ali (d)

Englewood Cliffs, N.J., March 7, 1967

90776	NUMBER ONE	Impulse IA 9360
90777	OGUNDE VARERE	(67) Impulse AS9120

Prob. Englewood Cliffs, N.J., March 29, 1967

90784	NUMBER EIGHT	unissued
90785	NUMBER SEVEN	"
90786	NUMBER SIX	"
90787	NUMBER FIVE	"
90788	NUMBER FOUR	"
90789	NUMBER TWO	"

Pharaoh Sanders (as), Algie DeWitt (perc) added

Prob. Englewood Cliffs, N.J., May 17, 1967

90790	NONE OTHER	unissued
90791	COLLIDOSCOPE	"

Note: EXPRESSION (issued on Impulse AS9120 (67)) does not correspond to 90776, but is a retitling of another piece from this last group of sessions, probably recorded May 17, 1967.

Album Index

Recently obtainable albums are shown here with American catalogue numbers first (if available) and, where different, European issues afterwards; basic recommended albums are those **printed in bold type.** Since continued availability is always a problem, it is advisable to use a knowledgeable jazz record shop such as those that advertise in jazz periodicals, and they may often be able to locate second-hand items as well.

(1) Durium (I) BLJ8039
(2) Duke (I) D1019
(3) Savoy (F) WL70517 (2)
(3a) Krazy Kat KK 7432
(3b) Krazy Kat KK 7431
(4) Verve (F) 2304.450
(5) CBS (F) 22132
(6) **CBS (F) 62323**
(7) CBS (F) 21070
(8) Prestige OJC-006, (F) 68.317
(9) Milestone M-47037
(10) Prestige P-24034, (F) 68.312
(10a) Prestige P-24001, (F) 68.311, (CD) VDJ 1503/1512
(10b) Prestige (CD) VDJ 1514
(11) Prestige P-24084
(11a) Prestige PR7150, (F) 68.400
(12) Prestige P-24104, (G) 0081.123
(12a) **Milestone M-47011, (F) 68.105**
(13) Prestige P-24059, (F) 68.359
(13a) Prestige OJC-079
(14) Prestige P-24069, (F) 68.351
(14a) Prestige P-24110
(15) Prestige P-24012, RCA (E) OJCD502
(15a) Prestige OJC-020, (CD) VDJ 1511
(16) Prestige (F) 68.343
(17) Riverside OJC-084
(18) Jazzland OJC-039, (F) 68.912, (CD) VDJ 1510
(19) Prestige P-24094, (F) 68.420
(20) **Prestige P-24003, (I) HB6002**
(20a) Prestige (F) 68.374
(21) **Blue Note BST81577**
(21a) Prestige P-24023
(22) Prestige P-24090
(23) Affinity (E) AFF106
(23a) Prestige P-24098
(24) Prestige P-24037, (F) 68.335
(25) Prestige OJC-021, (CD) VDJ 1502
(25a) Savoy (G) WL70529, (CD) ZD 70529
(26) Prestige OJC-078, (F) 68.344
(27) CBS (D) 85583
(28) Savoy SJL 1110
(29) Savoy (G) WL 70518, (CD) ZD 70518
(30) CBS (D) 85557
(30a) CBS (D) 88605
(31) Prestige P-24056, (F) 68.332
(31a) CBS (D) 85585
(32) Boplicity BOP1
(32a) Reactivation (E) JR147
(33) Mercury (D) 6336.319
(34) **CBS (E) 62066**

(34a) Atlantic 90416-1-Y
(35) **Atlantic (G) ATL50239**
(35a) Dragon DRLP 90/91
(35b) Unique Jazz (I) UJ19
(36) Atlantic (G) ATL50523
(36a) **Atlantic (F) 40278**
(37) **Atlantic (F) 40288**
(37a) CBS (F) 62104
(38) **Jasmine (E) JAS8**
(39) Jasmine (E) JAS59
(40) Atlantic (F) ATL40286
(40a) Impulse (I) AIMPL25013
(41) **Jasmine (E) JAS9**
(42) **Jasmine (E) JAS39**
(43) Beppo (E) BEP504
(44) Affinity (E) AFF14
(45) Jasmine (E) JAS37
(46) Affinity (E) AFF79
(46a) Musidisc (F) 30JA5184
(47) Jasmine (E) JAS10
(48) Jasmine (E) JAS4
(48a) Pablo 2308.217
(49) Duke (I) D1016
(50) Musidisc (F) 30JA5242 (N.B. (46a) and (50) comprise Festival (F) ALB378)
(51) **Jasmine (E) JAS11**
(52) Affinity (E) AFF16
(53) Pablo 2620.101
(54) Pablo 2310.886, (CD) 2310.886
(55) Pablo 2308.222
(56) Pablo 2308.227
(57) Jasmine (E) JAS41
(58) **MCA MCL1648**
(59) Impulse (I) IMPL5003
(60) Jasmine (E) JAS51
(61) **Jasmine (E) JAS45**
(62) Jasmine (E) JAS22
(62a) Jazz Masterworks CJZ LP1
(63) **Affinity (E) AFFD24**
(64) Impulse (I) AIMPL25042
(65) Jasmine (E) JAS80
(66) Jasmine (E) JAS16
(67) Jasmine (E) JAS73